THE DESIGN OF BICYCLE TRAILERS

Michael Ayre

New Edition

IT Publications 1986

Practical Action Publishing Ltd
27a Albert Street, Rugby, CV21 2SG, Warwickshire, UK
www.practicalactionpublishing.org

© Intermediate Technology Publications 1986

First published 1986
Reprinted in the UK, 2020
Reprinted by Practical Action Publishing
Rugby, Warwickshire UK

ISBN 9780946688975

All rights reserved. No part of this publication may be reprinted or reproduced or utilized in any form or by any electronic, mechanical, or other means, now known or hereafter invented, including photocopying and recording, or in any information storage or retrieval system, without the written permission of the publishers.

A catalogue record for this book is available from the British Library.

Since 1974, Practical Action Publishing has published and disseminated books and information in support of international development work throughout the world. Practical Action Publishing is a trading name of Practical Action Publishing Ltd (Company Reg. No. 1159018), the wholly owned publishing company of Practical Action. Practical Action Publishing trades only in support of its parent charity objectives and any profits are covenanted back to Practical Action (Charity Reg. No. 247257, Group VAT Registration No. 880 9924 76).

CONTENTS

	Page No.
Preface	iv
Introduction	v

1.	THE BICYCLE TRAILER	1
	Characteristics of Bicycle Trailers	1
	Performance of Bicycle Trailers	1
2.	DESIGN - GENERAL CONSIDERATIONS	3
	Introduction	3
	The Bicycle	3
	Single and Two Wheeled Bicycle Trailers	3
	Materials, Components and Equipment	4
3.	THE HITCH MECHANISM	7
	Function of the Hitch Mechanism	7
	Location of the Hitch	7
	Hitch Designs	11
4.	THE FRAME	29
	Size of the Frame	29
	Configuration of the Frame	29
	Frame Materials	30
	Frame Designs	31
5.	LOAD CONTAINERS	43
	Introduction	43
	Load Container Materials	43
	Load Container Designs	45
6.	WHEELS	55
	Introduction	55
	Requirements - Bicycle Trailer Wheels	55
	Attachment of Wheels to the Frame	55
	Commercially Available Wheels	56
	Wheel Designs	59

7.	USE OF BICYCLE TRAILERS	65
	Introduction	65
	Loading and Unloading	65
	Stability	65
	Maintenance	65

Annex 1: Commercial Suppliers of Bicycle Trailers and Components

Annex 2: Further Reading

PREFACE

This publication replaces a report, titled "The Design of Cycle Trailers", originally prepared in 1977 by the Transport Panel of the Intermediate Technology Development Group (ITDG). The report, by Ian Barwell, who is now an Executive Director of I.T. Transport Ltd., was produced as a limited circulation 'Information Paper'. The paper generated considerable interest, and was reprinted a number of times. Continuing interest, plus new research and manufacturing projects executed by I.T. Transport Ltd., have resulted in this new version of the original document.

M. Ayre
May 1986

INTRODUCTION

The bicycle is the most common wheeled vehicle in the world. Because of its efficiency, low-cost and versatility, the bicycle is extensively used in developing countries for personal transport and for the movement of goods. A variety of different methods are used in rural and urban areas to carry loads on bicycles, but the weight and volume that can be carried in safety is limited by the strength of the machine, and by problems of stability and control. The bicycle trailer has considerable potential for meeting many local transport needs in developing countries because of the following characteristics:

- It offers considerable flexibility because it is easily detachable from the bicycle;

- It allows heavy and voluminous loads to be transported safely by bicycle;

- It can be manufactured locally and purchased by bicycle owners to increase the utility of their vehicles.

Two-wheeled cycle trailers are common in certain parts of Europe but are rarely used in the developing world. The evidence indicates that this is not because the technology is inappropriate, but because it is unknown.

The intention of this publication is to provide basic design information for people in developing countries who wish to build bicycle trailers. However, it is not possible or desirable to specify a single unique trailer design which would be appropriate across the whole range of conditions and resources which are encountered in different parts of the world. Therefore, the approach which has been adopted is to analyse the critical aspects of trailer design and to discuss a number of alternative design solutions. Working with this information, a suitable trailer design can be developed which is effective in a specific set of circumstances.

The first section discusses the overall characteristics and performance of bicycle trailers. This is followed by an examination of some of the general issues which affect the development of a bicycle trailer design, and sections which analyse specific parts of a trailer - the hitch mechanism, the frame, load containers and wheels. The final section deals with the use of bicycle trailers. Annex 1 gives details of commercial suppliers of bicycle trailers and components. Annex 2 provides data on further sources of information.

1. THE BICYCLE TRAILER

Characteristics of Bicycle Trailers

Bicycle trailers enable a standard bicycle to move substantial loads, but can be easily and quickly detached when the cycle is required for personal transport. The trailer can also be used as a hand cart. However, all efficient, safe bicycle trailers share a number of important features:

- A mechanism which allows free rotational movement between the cycle and trailer when cornering, etc., but prevents any free play in the joint which would cause 'snatching' between the cycle and trailer.

- A simple and effective method of detaching/attaching the trailer.

- A strong and durable frame/load container.

- Wheel(s) which are capable of withstanding the loads imposed by regular use on rough or uneven roads.

- An overall configuration which ensures that the trailer does not affect the normal handling of the bicycle.

These characteristics are, in effect, the basic requirements of a well designed trailer. The following Sections discuss each of these requirements in detail, and suggest optional methods of meeting them.

Performance of Bicycle Trailers

The performance of a bicycle and trailer is governed by a number of factors - road conditions, age and health of the rider, weight of the load, quality and condition of the equipment, etc. However, there are some fundamental features of bicycle trailers which need to be considered when selecting the most appropriate form of transport for a given application:

- Bicycle trailers are very manoeuverable and should not affect the operation or handling of the bicycle. If well designed, a trailer does not apply a significant load to the bicycle but carries virtually all the weight on its own wheels.

- Trailers are, by definition, attached but not rigidly connected to the towing vehicle. All trailers, including those towed by motor vehicles, can be tipped over if pulled carelessly or too fast. Bicycles and trailers are quite safe when ridden properly, but the rider must develop the necessary control skills.

- In order to be safe, two wheeled trailers should not be loaded far in excess of the combined weight of the bicycle and rider. In practical terms, this means a **maximum payload of about 150 kg.** However, experience shows that trailers, like all other vehicles in developing countries, are often over-loaded, and it is sensible to include a safety factor of 2 - 2.5 in the design which will anticipate loads of up to 375 kg. This will minimise the dangers of over-loading by ensuring that the trailer itself does not fail, but the serious effects of carrying too much weight, in terms of balance, braking and stability must be recognised. Safe loads for a single wheeled trailer are discussed in Section 2.

The force required to pull and stop a fully loaded trailer makes a number of demands on the bicycle that is used. It is clearly important that the bicycle is in good general condition, but there are certain specific requirements which are essential if the bicycle and trailer are to be used safely and effectively.

Well maintained brakes are the most important requirement. It is possible to provide brakes on the trailer itself, but the complexity of such a feature would make the trailer more difficult to detach and significantly more expensive. The chain and sprockets of the bicycle should also be in good condition. One other option, which may be considered when a trailer is in constant use to carry heavy loads, is to replace the standard rear wheel sprocket with a larger one. This will reduce the gear ratio and therefore the effort required.

The use of a parking stand will enable the bicycle to be parked upright when attached to the trailer, and therefore make loading and unloading straightforward and safe.

2. DESIGN - GENERAL CONSIDERATIONS

Introduction

The choice of a suitable design of cycle trailer for a particular application will depend on a number of factors, including the fabrication skills and equipment which are available, the materials and components which can easily be obtained, the conditions under which the trailer will be used, and the type of load which it is expected to carry. The trailer may be required for a specific use, such as the transport of passengers or the movement of a particular type of cargo, or it may be needed as a general-purpose goods carrier. This Section examines the general issues to be considered when designing a trailer.

The Bicycle

The starting point for any bicycle trailer is the cycle with which it is to be used. If a 'one off' trailer is to be made to fit a specific bicycle, this does not cause any significant design problems. However, if trailers are to be manufactured in quantity, differences in the design and size of the bicycles which will be used with the trailers needs to be considered. These differences can be surprisingly marked. Conventional, large wheeled bicycles tend to look the same, but a closer inspection often reveals differences in frame construction, size, wheel mounting, frame geometry, saddle type, etc. All of these factors can affect the use of a bicycle with a specific trailer, and, in particular, the mounting of the hitch mechanism. It is therefore worthwhile to examine carefully, and preferably obtain data on, the type(s) of bicycle which will be used with the trailer that is to be developed. Particular attention should be given to the frame sizes available, the form and construction of the rear half of the frame, and the types of saddle in common use. Popular accessories should also be considered, including the type of frame lock which is attached above the rear wheel, carriers and parking stands.

Single and Two Wheeled Bicycle Trailers

Bicycle trailers are usually two wheeled devices and the main emphasis in the following sections is on this type. These are versatile, can carry reasonably heavy and/or bulky loads and are very easy to use. However, two wheeled trailers can be unsuitable for use on very narrow paths, as the additional width of the trailer, and the position of the wheels, may not fit into the narrow space available.

An innovative approach to this problem is the use of a single wheeled trailer which retains the 'single track' characteristics of the bicycle. They do, however, have the disadvantage of a lower capacity. A safe load for a single wheeled trailer is considered to be in the region of 80kg. They can, however, be used to carry very large, low density loads like straw or grass, and in common with two wheeled trailers, be used as hand carts.

A review of the uses to which the trailer will be put should provide information on what type of trailer - single or two wheeled - is required. A careful study of the uses of the proposed trailer will also provide useful data on its overall size.

Materials, Components and Equipment

Specific material and component requirements for each design are discussed in the following sections. However, it is worth noting the properties of some of the more commonly available materials, and the factors affecting the selection of components. The notes on equipment are intended to give a general outline of the facilities required to produce the designs shown in the following sections.

Materials

In general, steel is a very suitable material for bicycle trailer construction. It has a very good strength to weight ratio; is available in a wide range of forms and sizes; and is easy to work with. The most common types of steel for bicycle trailer construction are lightweight mild steel tube, which is usually referred to as Electric Resistance Welded (ERW) or 'furniture' tube; mild steel angle iron; mild steel round bar; mild steel strip and mild steel sheet. It is important to select the correct specification, in terms of strength, for the intended use, and examine carefully the quality of material to be used. This is particularly important for tubular steel, as quality, and hence strength, can vary widely.

Wood is a useful material for load containers, and in many countries, an inexpensive solution. Wood framed bicycle trailers have been produced in Europe, but these designs are not included in this publication, as the strength and durability of an acceptably light wood framed trailer is unlikely to be sufficient to meet the stresses imposed by heavy use on rough roads.

Glass Reinforced Plastic (GRP), which is more commonly known as 'Fibreglass', is suitable for load containers, but difficult to obtain in many countries, and expensive and difficult to repair without suitable facilities. However, it is well suited to some specialist containers, particularly if the load needs to be kept cold or effective cleaning (food, milk, etc.) is required.

Components

A number of "bought in" components are specified in the designs in the following sections. There are three essential requirements of any component used in a bicycle trailer design:

   i) It should be durable enough to meet the loads and forces imposed on the trailer;

   ii) It should be easily available in the market place;

   iii) It should be easily repairable, and any required spare parts should be available in the areas where the trailer is to be used. This is particularly important when a component is expected to require repair or replacement due to normal wear, ie. spokes and tyres.

In addition to these factors, the cost and weight of a component will need to be considered. Cost is particularly important, as the "bought in" components can form a significant proportion of the sales price of a bicycle trailer.

Equipment

The trailer designs described in this publication require basic metal working facilities. These can be summarized as:

Cutting:	Hacksaw - powered or hand operated.
Tube bending:	Tube bending equipment - hand operated.
Metal bending:	Forge or Oxy-Acetylene equipment.
Drilling:	Power drill, preferably mounted on a stand.
Welding:	Oxy-Acetylene, Electric Arc or Metal Inert Gas (MIG).
Sheet metal:	Shears, folding equipment, spot welder or rivetting equipment.
Turning:	Simple lathe.
Painting:	Paint spraying facilities.
Hand tools:	Files, spanners, hammers, etc.

Some of the designs do not require all this equipment. A number, for example, do not require sheet metal forming tools or a lathe.

The manufacture of bicycle trailers in quantity will require additional equipment in order to simplify the production process, maximise efficiency and finish the product to a high standard. The development of welding jigs and fixtures, for example, will ensure the accuracy and consistency of production and minimise manufacturing time. Good quality painting equipment, and a clean area in which to use it, will help to ensure a high quality finish.

3. THE HITCH MECHANISM

Function of the Hitch Mechanism

The hitch mechanism is, in many ways, the most important part of a bicycle trailer. The hitch connects the trailer to the bicycle and allows free rotational movement in certain directions when cornering, going over rough ground, etc.. However, it should not allow significant free play or slack which could create 'snatching' between the cycle and the trailer.

Two wheeled trailers require a hitch mechanism which allows rotation about three axes (Fig. 3.1). Single wheeled trailers, however, need to be held upright by the bicycle and, in turn, by the riding action of the user (Fig. 3.2). This requirement complicates the design of hitches for single wheeled trailers, as they need to be capable of withstanding the considerable torsional forces generated by the load when cornering.

The second function of the hitch mechanism is to allow the trailer to be attached to or detached from the bicycle quickly, safely, and easily. This function is central to the versatility and convenience of a bicycle trailer, as it ensures that the owner can detach the trailer when it is not needed. Ideally, the method of attaching/detaching should not require any tools and should not involve removing any parts of the hitch for any length of time, as these may be mislaid.

Location of the Hitch

Normally, one part of the hitch mechanism is permanently attached to the bicycle, and another to the trailer. The part which is attached to the bicycle should be securely and rigidly fitted. The majority of hitches described in this section are located on the frame directly below the saddle and use the seat lug bolt or the seat stays as the point of attachment. This is the recommended position, as it locates the hitch within the wheelbase of the bicycle. Some designs exist which position the hitch behind the axle line of the rear wheel. This is considered to be unsuitable, as normal loading of the trailer can cause downward pressure on the hitch which will tend to lift the front wheel of the cycle.

Rear carriers are very popular in some countries and are extremely useful for carrying relatively small loads. Some bicycle trailer designs mount the hitch above the carrier on the seat stays or use the carrier as the attachment point. If the hitch is mounted on the seat stays it is probable that the carrier will need to be removed, as it may interfere with the trailer frame during cornering or going over rough ground. However, this will depend on the type of carrier fitted, and the design of the trailer hitch and frame. Mounting a hitch on the rear of a carrier is not recommended, as most carriers are not strong enough and the mounting point will be behind the rear axle, resulting in the problems outlined above. The hitch designs on the following pages include one which uses the rear wheel axle as a mounting point. This design may be suitable if a rear carrier must be used with the bicycle.

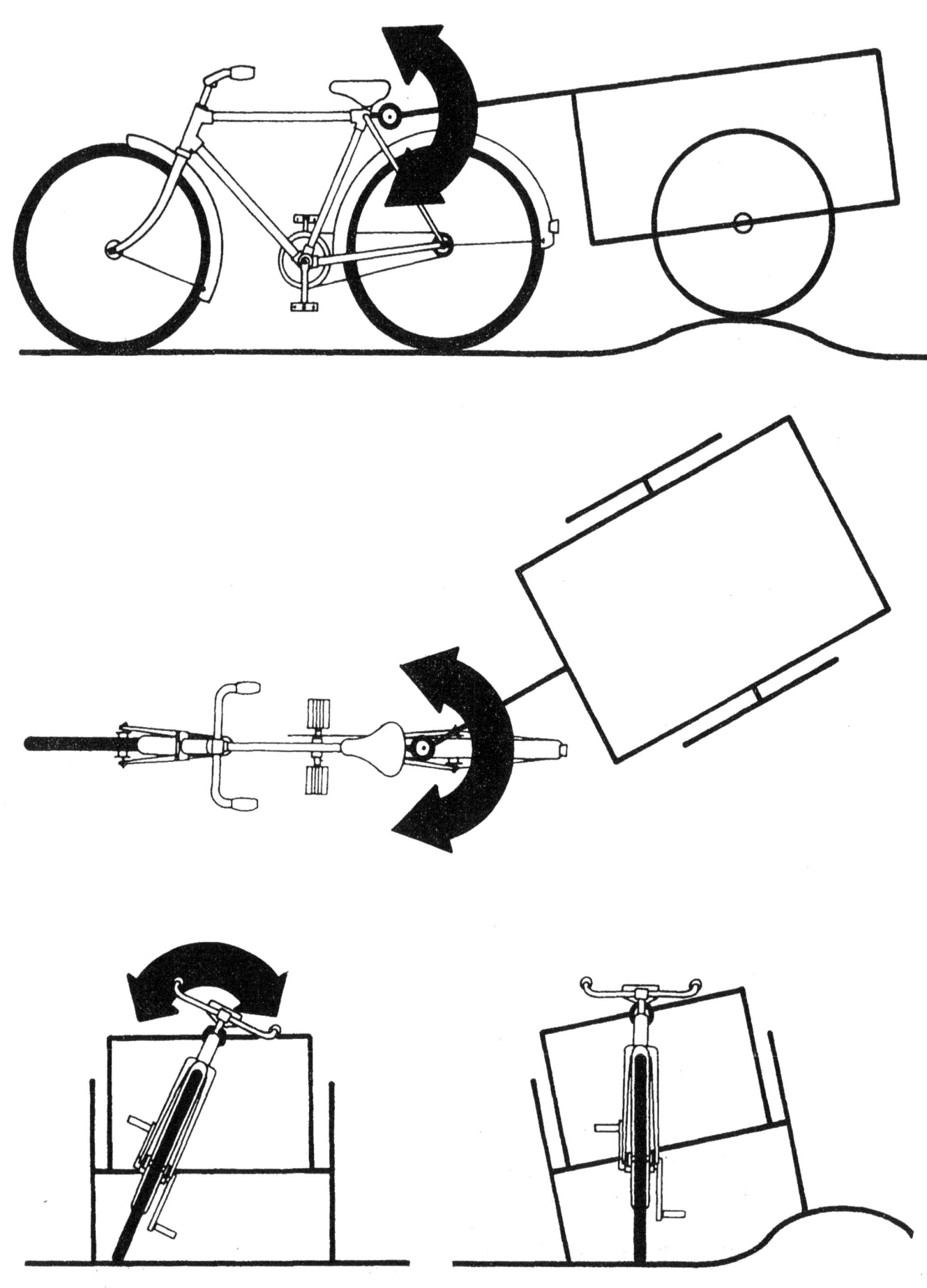

Figure 3.1: Rotational Requirements of a Two Wheeled Trailer Hitch

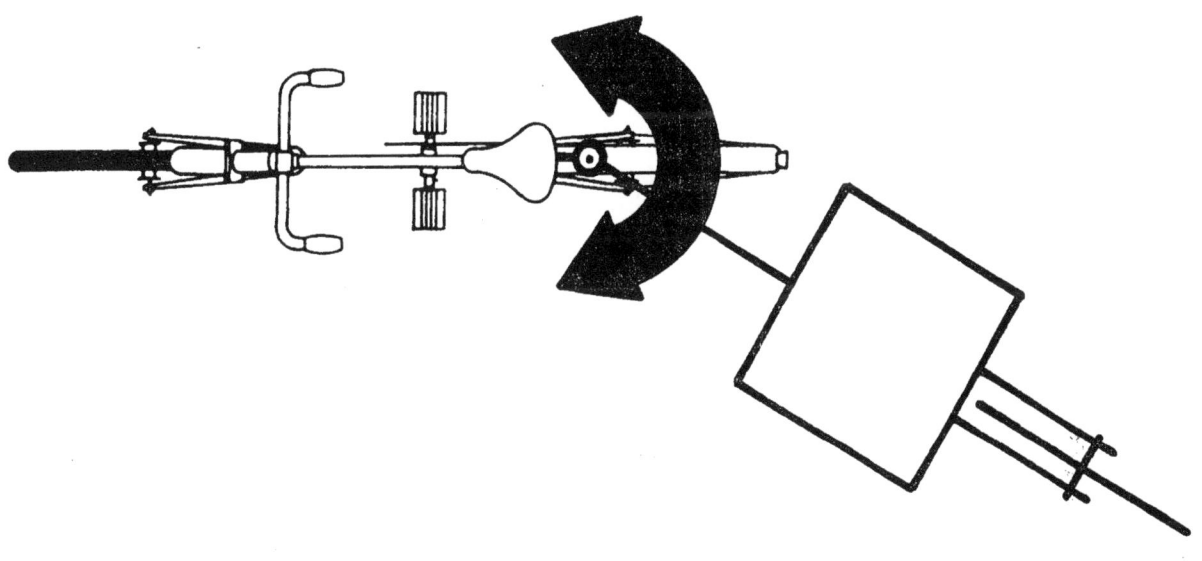

Figure 3.2: Rotational Requirements of a Single Wheeled Trailer Hitch

If the hitch is to be mounted beneath the saddle, the size and configuration of the bicycle seat stays and the design and position of the saddle will affect the space available. As discussed in Section 2, it is worthwhile spending some time examining the bicycle(s) which are to be used with the proposed trailer before deciding on a particular design. If the configuration of the seat stays/saddle is not taken into account, the free movement of the trailer relative to the bicycle may be limited, which could be dangerous.

Hitch Designs

The following eight designs are either commercially available products, which will normally be sold as part of a complete trailer, or examples of hitches which have been developed for locally produced trailers in developing countries. The information is presented in the following way:

- A detailed drawing of each hitch.

- A description of each hitch.

- A list of materials and components required.

- A list of production equipment needed.

- A brief analysis of the design which notes disadvantages and advantages.

- Information on commercial examples if applicable.

The designs shown cover a wide technology range, from very basic to relatively sophisticated. The information given in this Section should be combined with subsequent data on frames, load containers and wheels in order to select or develop a suitable design of trailer.

Hitch Design 1 - Rubber Hose (UK)

Description: This design uses a flexible rubber hose to provide the necessary rotational movement between the bicycle and trailer. The rubber hose is subjected to considerable loads in use. It is therefore recommended that high strength steel reinforced hose, of the type normally used on hydraulic or compressed air equipment is used.

The hitch is clamped to the bicycle using a 'U' clamp which fits around the seat post of the bicycle. This needs to be tightened carefully in order to avoid damage to the lightweight tube of the seat post.

The trailer is attached to the bicycle using a 'T' shaped steel pin which passes through the hose and the round bar which is welded to the trailer.

The 'T' shaped pin should be at least 5mm in diameter, as it is subjected to considerable forces during use.

Materials/
Components: 'U' clamp, hose clip, steel reinforced hose, mild steel round bar.

Production
Equipment: Cutting, welding, drilling.

Advantages: Simplicity; complete absence of any free play or 'snatching'; simple attachment/detachment.

Disadvantages: Requires clamping to seat post which limits the adjustment of the saddle height; rubber hose may not be durable in some climates.

Commercial
Example: Designed and manufactured by Bike Hod Ltd. (see Annex 1).

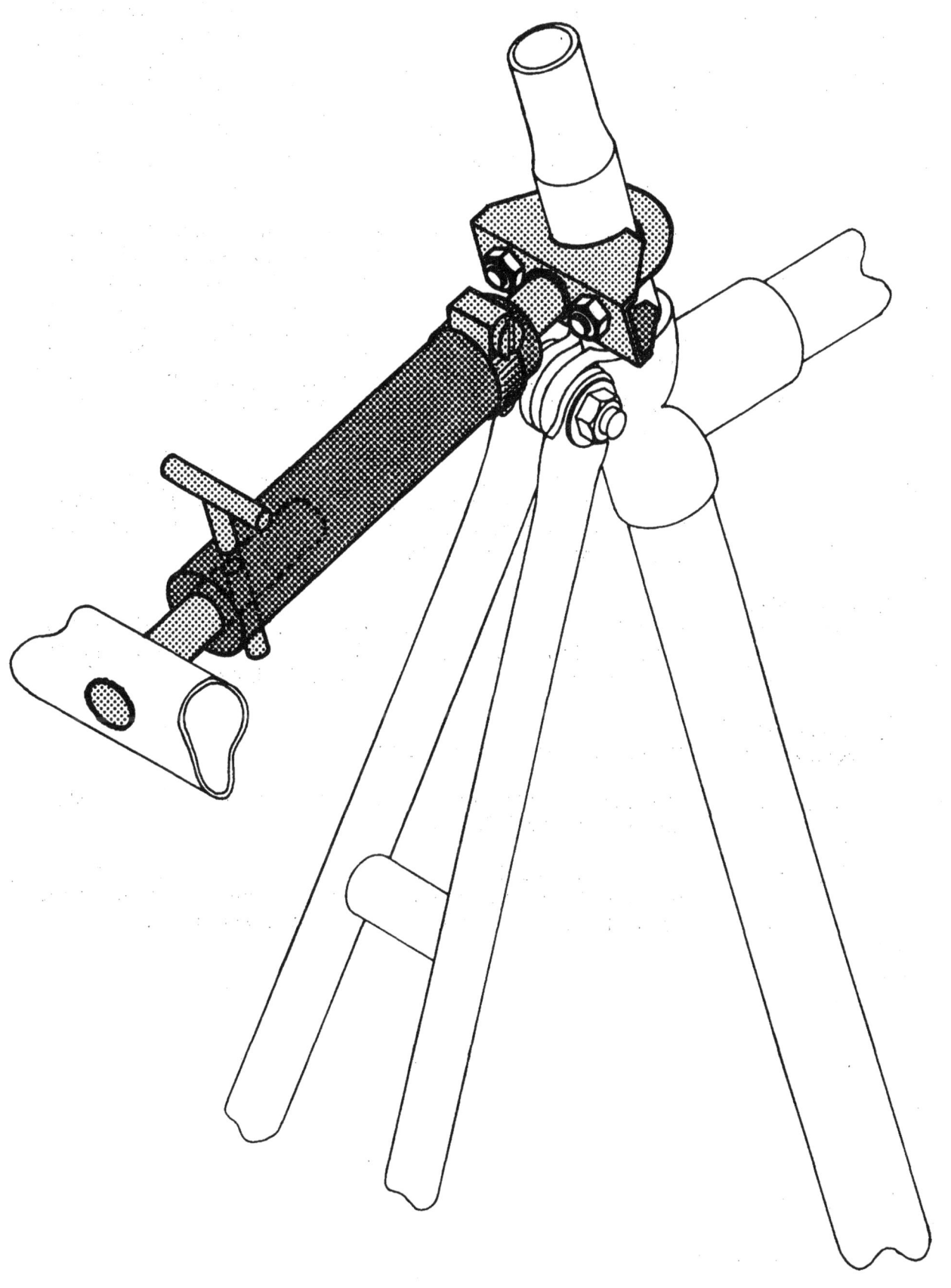

Hitch Design 2 – Castor (Papua New Guinea)

Description: This hitch incorporates part of a standard castor wheel to provide the required rotational movement. The ball bearings in the castor pivot act as a thrust bearing, which makes the hitch particularly suitable for heavy loads. This type of hitch performs well except for very minor 'snatching' at the pivot points, which may result in mechanical wear. This can be minimised by regular greasing.

The hitch is clamped to the seat stays, just below the saddle, using two plates. In order to maximise the contact area, and prevent damage to the seat stays, two rubber pads are fitted to the clamping surfaces. These pads should be the same size as the clamping plates and approximately 6mm thick. This will enable the hitch clamp to 'mould' itself around the seat stays, increasing the contact area and decreasing the chance of slip during use.

The trailer is attached to the bicycle by a round bar which fits through the pivot block on the hitch. This bar is located by a pin, preferably of the self-retaining spring type.

Materials/
Components: Furniture castor (wheel removed); mild steel strip, nuts, bolts, washers, mild steel round bar, spring steel pin; rubber pads; mild steel stock.

Production
Equipment: Cutting, welding, drilling.

Advantages: Reasonably efficient, with good rotational ability; easily attached/detached.

Disadvantages: Likely to require considerable space on seat stays – may not be suitable for a small framed bicycle; could be difficult to repair castor at village level.

Hitch Design 3 - Samaru Cart (Nigeria)

Description: This design uses a simple mechanical linkage - basically two interlocking steel loops - to provide the rotational movement required. The design is best suited to relatively light use, as there will be some free movement between the loops, which will result in 'snatching'.

The hitch is attached to the bicycle seat stays using two clamping plates. As illustrated, the plates are only clamped by one bolt. In practice, it may be necessary to re-design the clamping plates to provide two bolts, as in the previous design. As with other clamp plate designs, rubber pads will increase the contact area on the seat stays and protect the bicycle frame.

An interesting feature of the design is the spring loaded pin which attaches the trailer to the bicycle. By pushing against the end of the 'U' shaped pin, the two loops are disconnected. This system prevents the hitch pin being mislaid.

Materials/
Components: Mild steel round bar; mild steel strip; nut(s), bolt(s) and washers; a compression spring (to fit over the mild round bar); a steel pin (to hold the spring in place); rubber pads.

Production
Equipment: Cutting, welding, drilling, metal bending.

Advantages: Quick release mechanism with retained hitch pin; simplicity of construction.

Disadvantages: Mechanical free play which will cause 'snatching' between cycle and trailer; one bolt mounting (as illustrated).

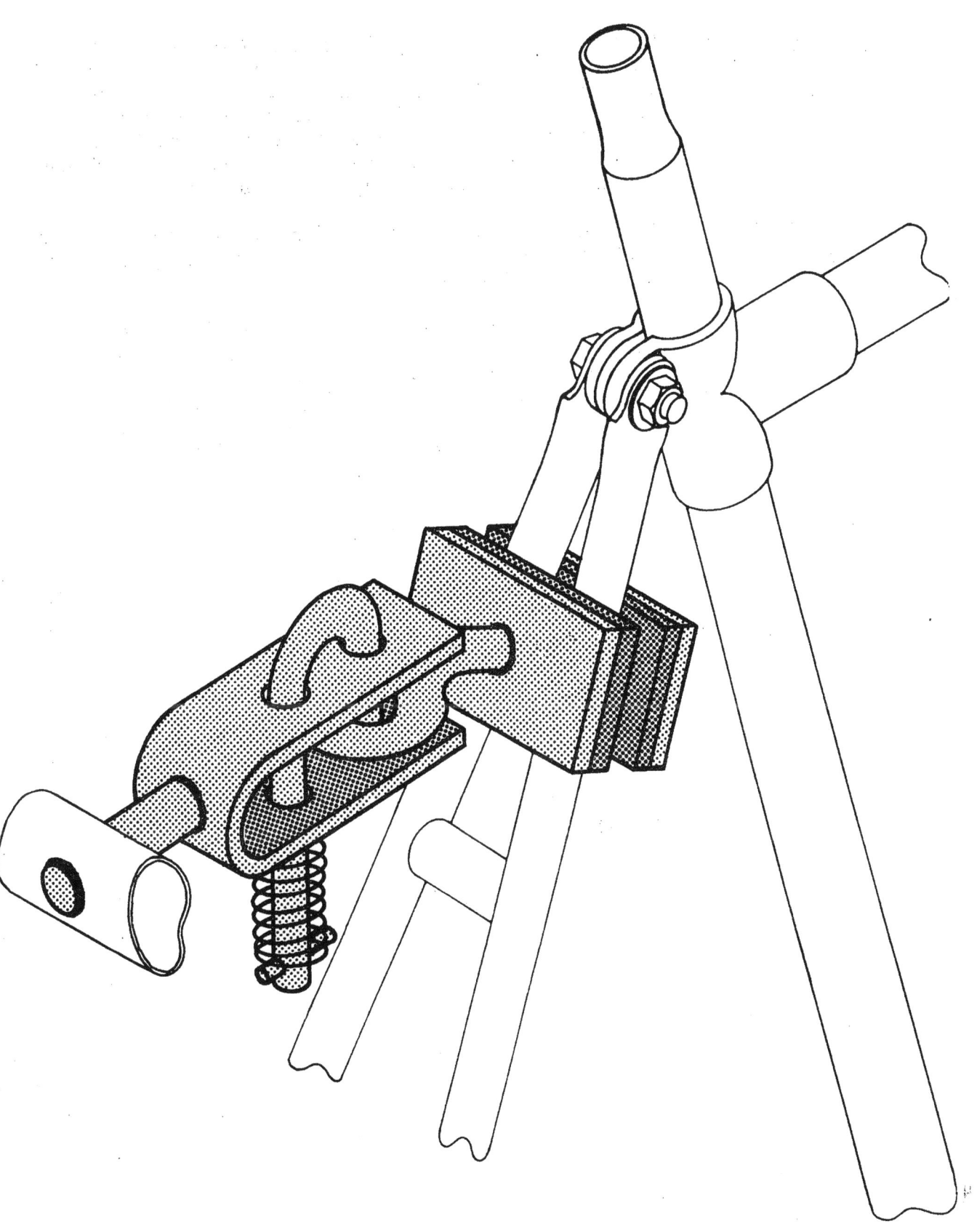

Hitch Design 4 - Rubber Strap (USA)

Description: This hitch, like Design 1, uses rubber to provide the necessary freedom of movement between the bicycle and the trailer. The design is essentially a strip of rubber which is clamped in place around the base of the seat post. To obtain the required strength, it is recommended that fabric reinforced rubber - which can be obtained from some scrap car tyres - is used.

The rubber strip should be clamped close to the seat post to prevent 'snatching', but be flexible enough to allow free rotational movement.

The trailer is attached to the bicycle using a 'T' shaped steel pin which passes through the steel tube welded to the clamp which holds the rubber in place, and the round bar welded to the trailer frame.

The 'T' shaped pin should be at least 5mm in diameter, as it is subjected to considerable forces during use.

Materials/
Components: Rubber strip (possibly cut from a scrap car tyre); nuts, bolts and washers; mild steel round bar; mild steel tube; mild steel strip; mild steel angle.

Production
Equipment: Cutting, welding, drilling.

Advantages: Simplicity; easy connection/disconnection; low cost.

Disadvantages: Requires clamping to seat post which limits the adjustment of the saddle height; rubber strip may not be durable in some climates; retaining pin may come out during use.

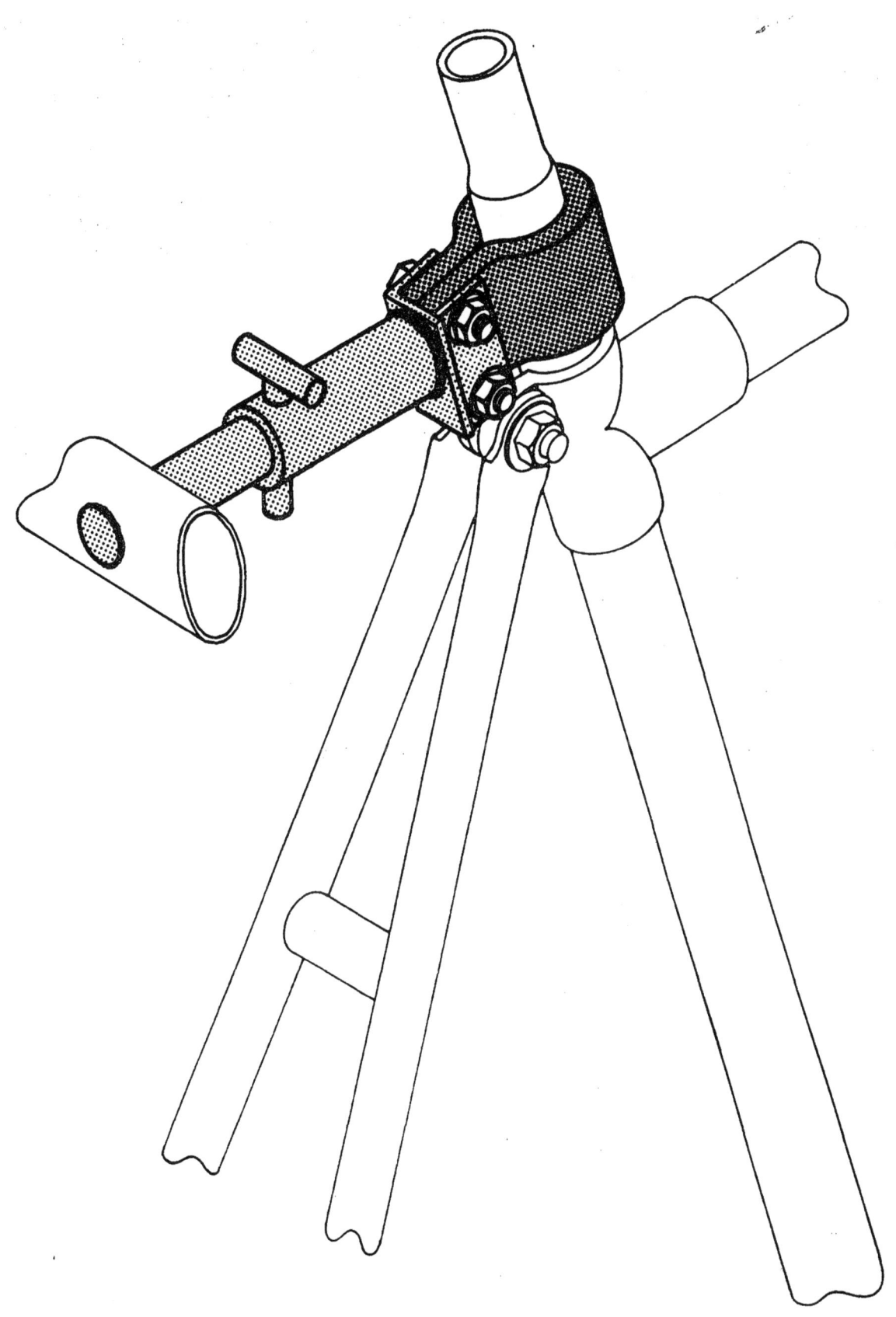

Hitch Design 5 - Loadstar (India)

Description: This design was developed by I.T. Transport Ltd. as part of a programme to establish the production of cycle trailers in India. The hitch is a 'heavy duty' design which uses a ball and socket arrangement to provide completely free rotational movement and prevent any 'snatching' between the bicycle and the trailer.

The hitch is attached by a plate which clamps the body of the mechanism to the seat stays of the bicycle. In common with other designs of this type, rubber pads are recommended to maximise contact area and protect the bicycle frame.

The trailer is attached to the bicycle by locating the hitch ball in the socket. The ball is retained by a high tensile steel bolt and wingnut.

Materials/Components: Mild steel stock (to produce the ball); mild steel strip; mild steel round bar; nuts, bolts, washers; high tensile steel bolt and wing nut; rubber pads.

Production Equipment: Cutting, welding, drilling, turning, metal bending.

Advantages: Durable, heavy duty design; simple to attach/detach; does not have any free play which would cause 'snatching'.

Disadvantages: Requires some machining to produce ball.

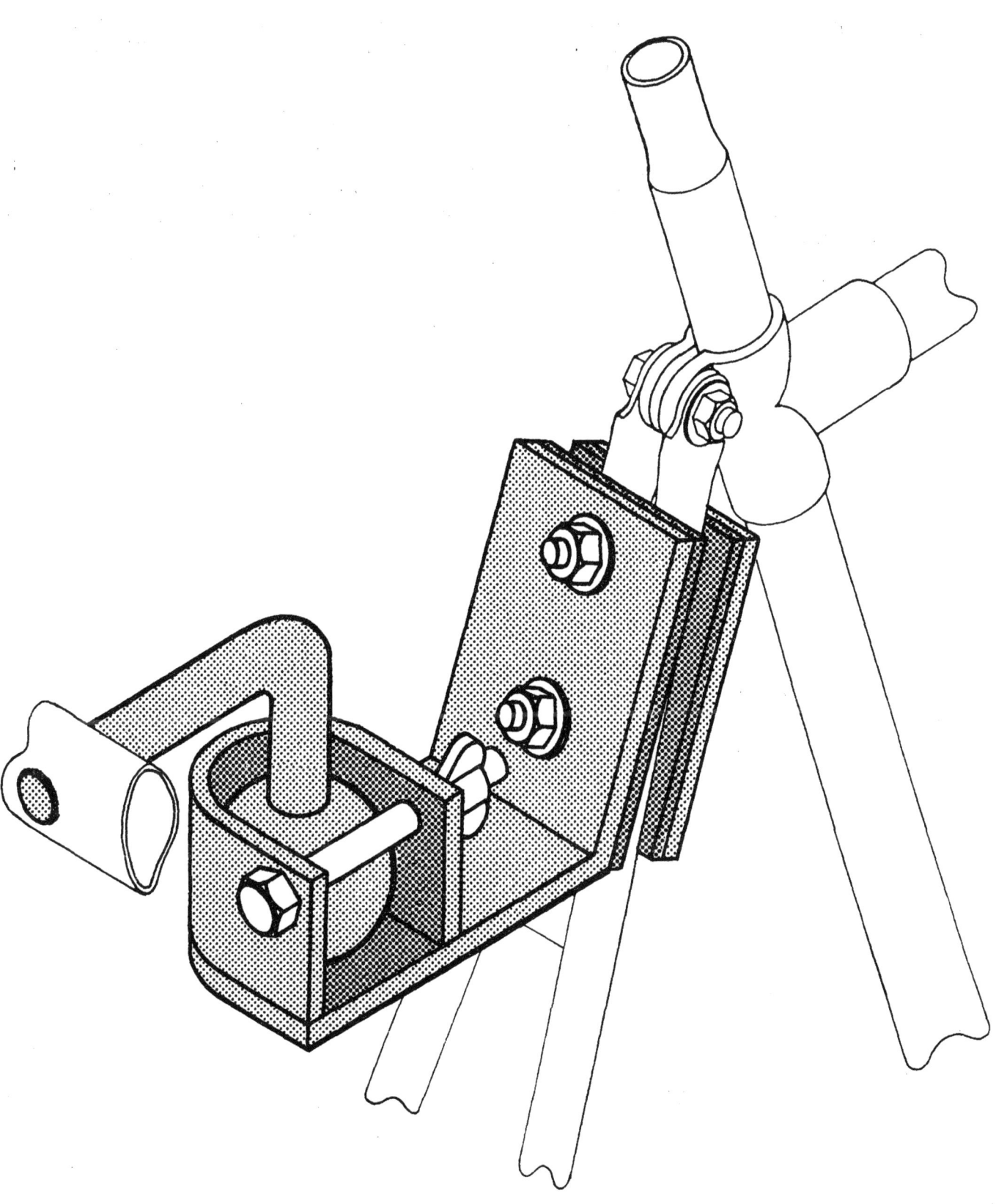

Hitch Design 6 (East Africa)

Description: This design uses a conventional 'universal' joint and a collar attached to the trailer frame to provide the required free rotational movement.

As illustrated, the hitch is attached to the bicycle frame seat stays by one bolt. As mentioned in the description of Design 3, one bolt is unlikely to be sufficient to retain a hitch effectively, particularly if the trailer is heavily used. It is recommended that the mounting is modified to accept two bolts. Rubber pads should be used between the clamping plates and the seat stays.

The trailer is attached to the bicycle by a 'T' shaped pin which passes through the hitch behind the collar on the trailer. The retaining pin should be at least 5mm in diameter, as it is subjected to considerable forces during use.

Materials/
Components: Mild steel stock (for universal joint blocks); mild steel strip; nut(s), bolt(s) and washers; mild steel round bar; mild steel tube.

Production
Equipment: Cutting, welding, drilling, turning.

Advantages: Simple attachment/detachment; does not have free play which would cause 'snatching'.

Disadvantages: Complex to produce; requires machining.

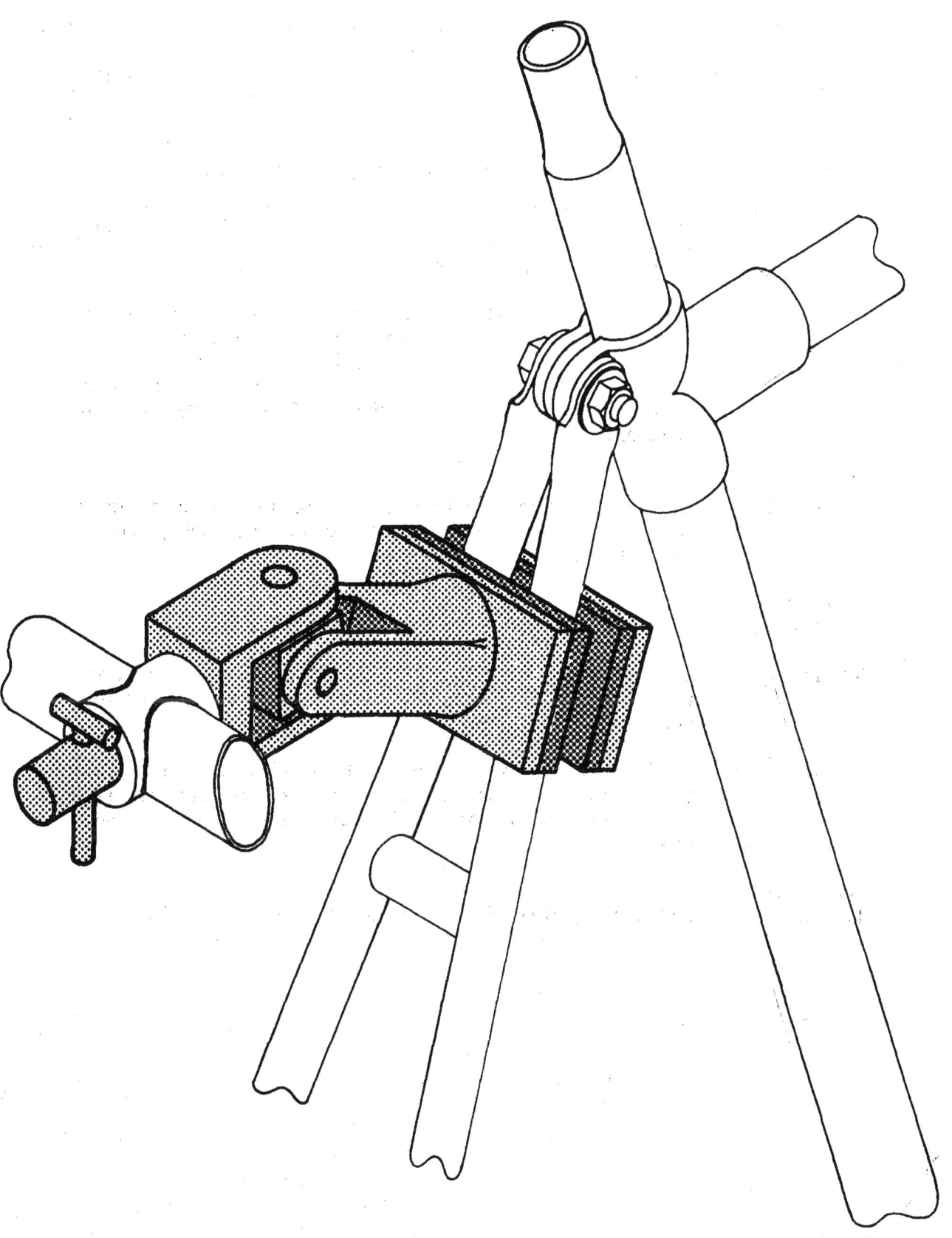

Hitch Design 7 - Shuttle (UK)

Description: This design uses the bicycle rear axle as the mounting point and requires a trailer configuration which is different from that used with Designs 1 - 6. An example of a suitable trailer is Frame Design 1. Rotational movement is provided by a rubber coupling which rotates about one axis in a retaining clamp and is flexible enough to allow movement along the other two axes.

The hitch is attached to the bicycle at the rear wheel axle. It is clamped around one of the chain stays in addition to the mounting over the rear axle.

The trailer is attached to the bicycle by opening the swing clamp. This is then closed around the rubber coupling and secured in position by a small padlock. This system provides a firm, 'snatch' free mounting with the additional advantage of security for the trailer.

Materials/
Components: Mild steel strip; mild steel round bar; shaped rubber coupling; retaining pin for coupling; nuts, bolts, washers; padlock.

Production
Equipment: Cutting, drilling, welding, metal bending.

Advantages: Bicycle can be used with rear carrier; simple construction; no free play which would cause 'snatching'; security.

Disadvantages: Trailer configuration cannot be easily used as a hand cart; rubber coupling may not be durable in some climates; cannot be used with some types of cycle stand.

Commercial
Example: Marketed by Woodland World Limited (see Annex 1).

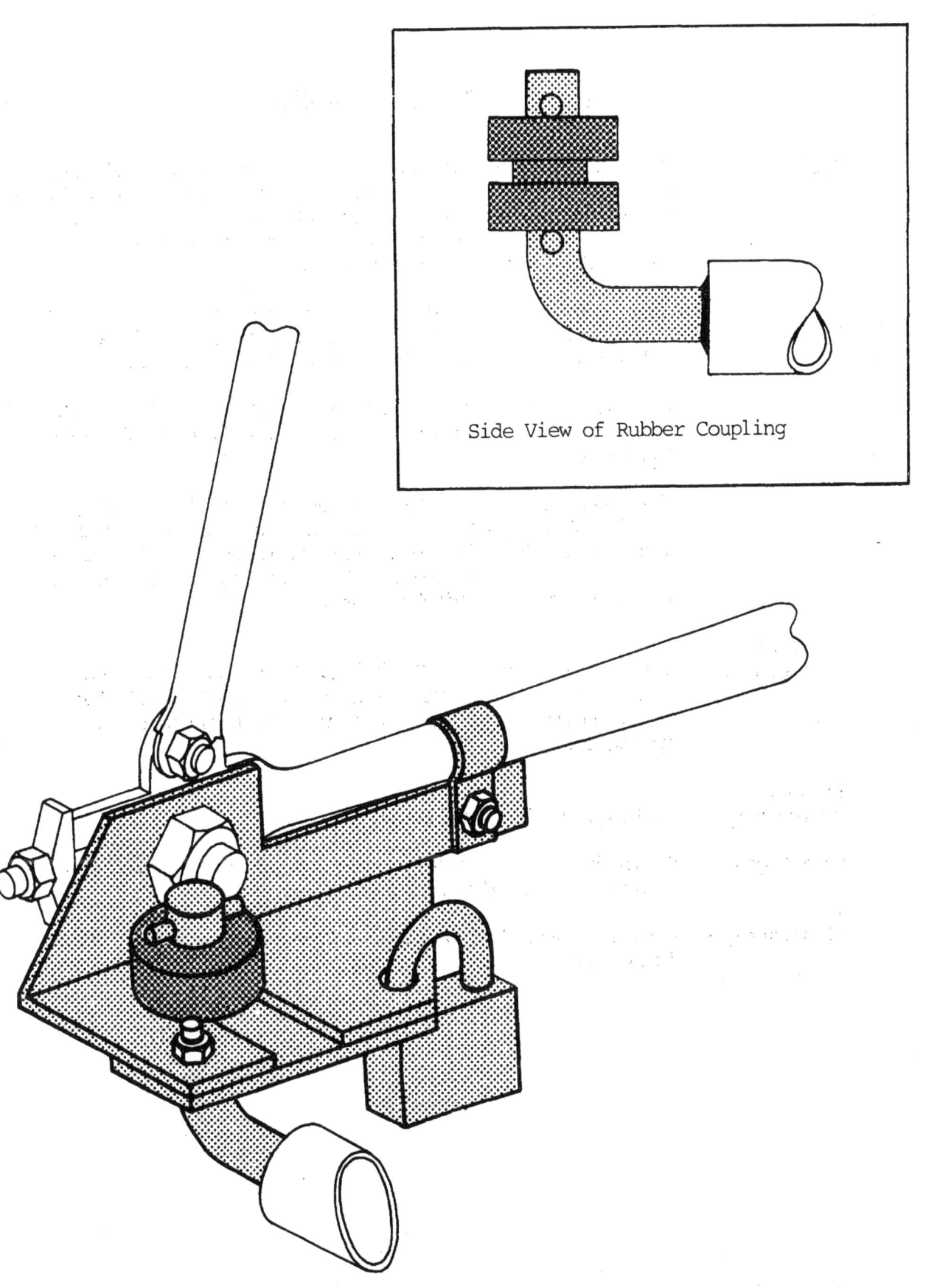

Side View of Rubber Coupling

25

Hitch Design 8 - Single Wheeled Trailer Hitch (UK)

Description: This design was developed by I.T. Transport Ltd. for use with the single wheeled trailer - Frame Design 5. As discussed at the beginning of this section, single wheeled trailers require a different type of hitch to those used with two wheeled devices.

The hitch illustrated allows the bicycle and trailer to go over bumps and to turn corners, but does not allow the trailer to tilt relative to the bicycle.

The hitch needs to be extremely stiff, and is both clamped around the seat lug and bolted through the seat lug clamp.

The trailer is attached to the bicycle by sliding a steel tube, which forms part of the trailer, over a section of bicycle handlebar stem which acts as a pivot. A steel pin, preferably of spring steel, retains the tube on the handlebar stem.

Materials/
Components: Mild steel strip; 2 ´U´ bolt clamps (´U´ bolts removed); bicycle handlebar stem; mild steel tube; nuts, bolts, washers; retaining pin (preferably of spring steel).

Production
Equipment: Cutting, welding, drilling.

Advantages: Rigid hitch for single wheeled trailer; trailer is easily attached/detached.

Disadvantages: Requires care during construction to ensure that there is no free play.

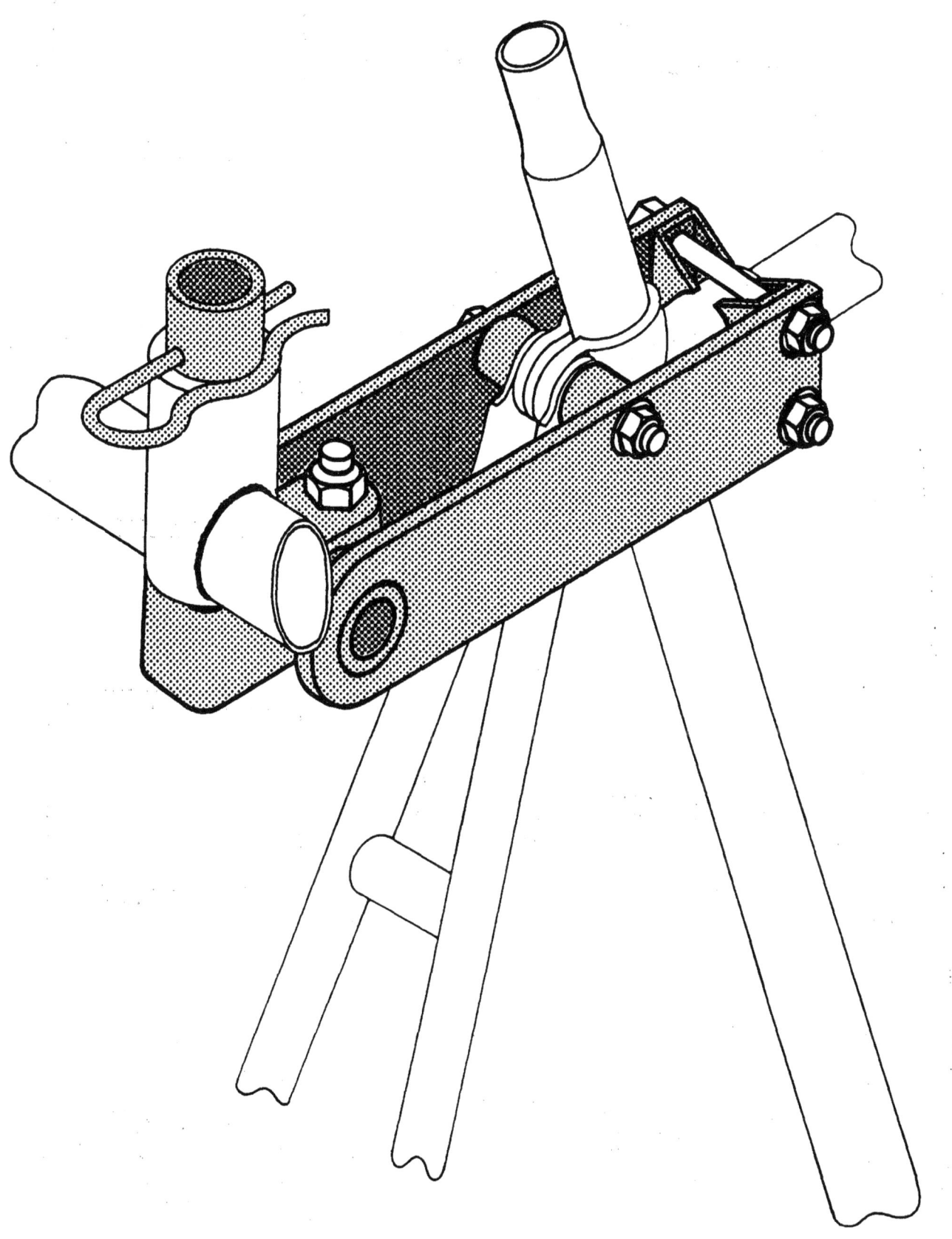

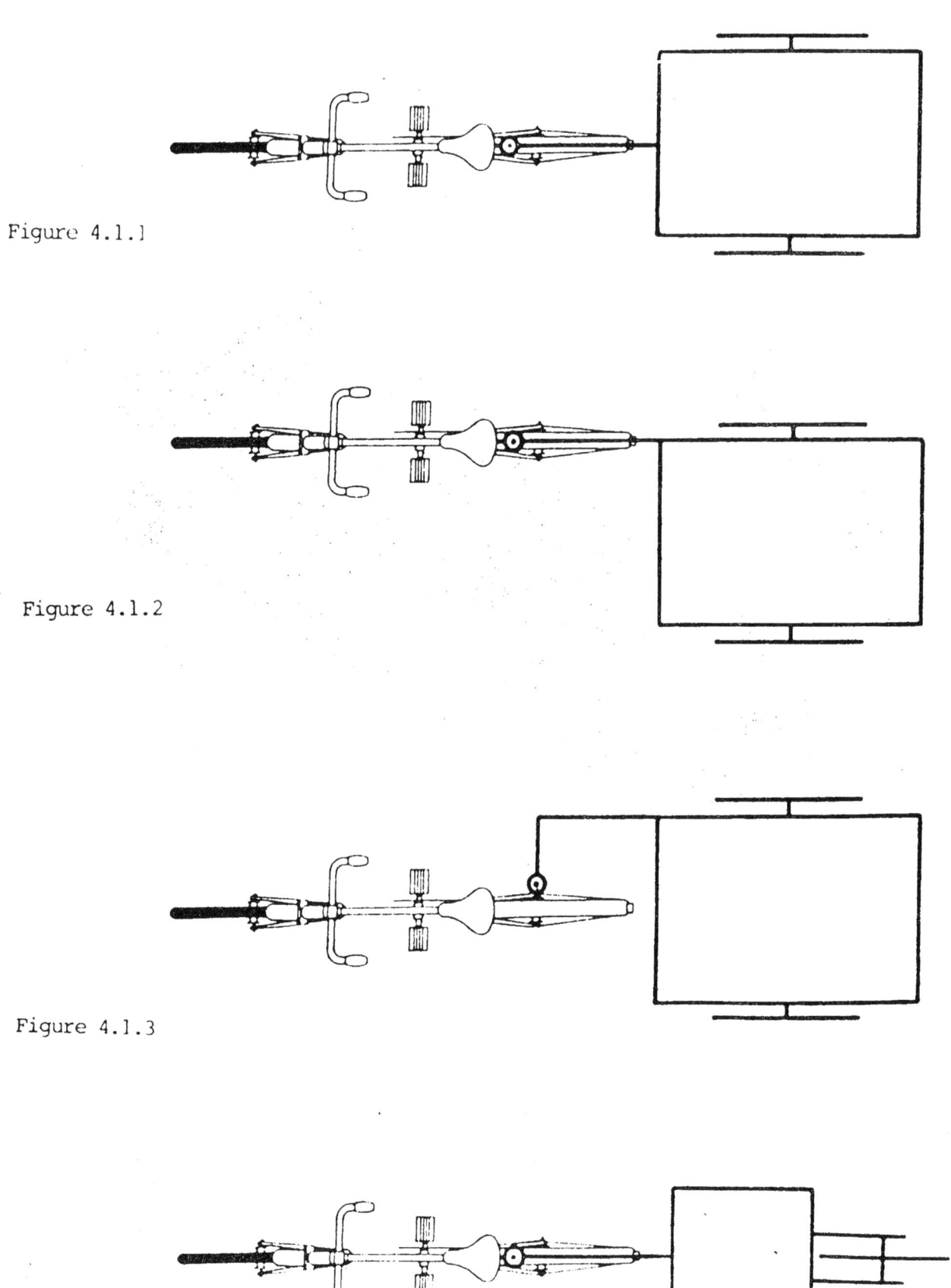

Figure 4.1.1

Figure 4.1.2

Figure 4.1.3

Figure 4.1.4

Figure 4.1: Configuration of Bicycle Trailer Frames

4. THE FRAME

Size of the Frame

The size of the trailer will depend on a number of factors - cost, loads to be carried, traffic regulations (if applicable), density of traffic in the expected area of use, road conditions, etc. The size should suit the dimensions of any standard containers which may be carried in the trailer. These include oil drums, milk churns, packing cases, etc. For example, a 200 litre oil drum may be very useful for carrying kerosene, water, etc.

A very large trailer may be unsafe in traffic and encourage overloading, which can cause frame failure and accidents. The maximum recommended load for a two wheeled trailer is, as previously discussed, 150 kg. However, if a trailer is too narrow, it will become unstable and may overturn.

The designs shown in this Section do not include dimensions, as these will depend on specific requirements. As an approximate guide, the following are considered to be **maximum** dimensions for a two wheeled trailer:

    Overall Width of Trailer: 900mm
    (including wheels)
    Overall Length of Load Container: 1000mm
    Overall depth of Load Container: 500mm

A single wheeled trailer should have a considerably smaller load area, as it is only capable of safely carrying loads of approximately 80 kg.

Configuration of the Frame

There are three suitable configurations for a two wheeled trailer. The standard configuration has the hitch mounted below the saddle and the trailer positioned symmetrically in plan view behind the bicycle (Figure 4.1.1). In some situations, it may be useful to have a trailer which is off-set from the bicycle, particularly if local roads are deeply rutted from the passage of other two or four wheeled vehicles. However, it should be noted that off-setting the trailer results in a lateral force being applied to the bicycle, which may affect handling and balance. (Figure 4.1.2). Another option is to attach the hitch to the rear axle, as illustrated in Hitch Design 7. This allows the standard or off-set trailer configuration (Figure 4.1.3). An allowance must be made for the cycle to turn relative to the trailer. This configuration enables a shorter tow bar to be used, and produces less lateral force on the cycle than the layout shown in (Figure 4.1.2). However, the trailer cannot be used as a hand cart, as the tow bar is mounted too low.

On a two wheeled trailer it is important to position the wheels correctly. As a general rule, the centre of gravity of the load should act just in front of the axle line of the trailer. This places a small downward force onto the bicycle, which contributes to the stability and safety of the trailer. Allowing the centre of gravity to act behind the axle line of the trailer may, under some circumstances, cause the rear wheel of the bicycle to lift, which is dangerous. In practical terms, the position of the centre of gravity will depend on the method of loading as well as the design of the trailer. But the design should encourage correct loading.

The only configuration for a single wheeled trailer which provides adequate stability and balance is shown in Figure 4.1.4. The hitch is mounted below the saddle, and the centre line of the wheel and frame is in line with the bicycle wheels. The load area of a single wheeled trailer should be low, and positioned in front of the wheel. This contributes to stability, and minimises the torsional loading on the trailer. Frame Design 7 shows a suitable layout.

Frame Materials

Mild Steel Tube

Round tubular steel with a thin (1.4mm - 1.8mm) wall section is a very suitable material for bicycle trailer frames. In some countries it is known as Electric Resistance Welded (ERW) tube, in others as Furniture Tube. It should not be confused with the lightweight tube used as electrical conduit, which has very little structural strength.

ERW tube can be bent, using a tube bending machine, to form simple, attractive frame components. It is easily welded, and does not require power cutting machines. The main advantage of the material is that it has a very high strength to weight ratio and considerable rigidity when formed into a frame. ERW tube is usually specified by the outside diameter and the wall thickness. 25 mm outside diameter is a common size, and this is specified for most of the following designs. Other sizes can, however, be substituted.

Mild Steel Angle

Angle iron is available in a range of sizes, two common ones being 25mm x 25mm x 3mm and 50mm x 50mm x 6mm. 25mm angle iron is a suitable material for bicycle trailer frames if tubular steel is not available. However, it has a lower strength to weight ratio than tube. Larger angle iron sections are not generally suitable for frames, as the weight will be unacceptably high.

Mild Steel Strip

Steel strip, like angle iron, is available in a wide range of sizes. Because of its lack of rigidity, it is not suitable for bicycle trailer frames, but can be used for some frame components.

Frame Designs

The following designs represent the most common types of bicycle trailer frame. Virtually all the designs shown are constructed from tubular steel. However, there is no reason why these designs should not be modified to suit angle iron or other materials. The emphasis on tubular steel designs simply reflects the suitability of the material for this application.

The information in this section is presented in the following way:

- A detailed drawing of each frame which shows the approximate dimensional relationship between bicycle and trailer.

- A description of each frame design.

- A list of materials and components required.

- A list of production equipment needed.

- A brief analysis of each design which notes advantages and disadvantages.

The information given in this section should be combined with data in Sections 2, 3, 5 and 6 to select or develop a suitable trailer design.

Frame Design 1 - Platform Frame

Description: This design is the most simple type of bicycle trailer frame. As illustrated, it is best suited to relatively lightweight loads (up to 80 kg). Transport of greater loads would require additional braces to be added to the tow bar and the base of the frame.

The frame is illustrated in two forms. The upper illustration shows a configuration suitable for a hub mounted hitch (Hitch Design 7). This configuration is also illustrated in Figure 4.1.4. As shown, the frame is designed for use with standard bicycle wheels (26" or 28" diameter) which allow the tow bar to be easily integrated into the frame. However, the position of the tow bar makes the trailer unsuitable for use as a hand-cart.

The lower illustration shows a more conventional configuration, suitable for use with Hitch Designs 1 - 6.

Although this design is shown in tubular steel, it would be simple to reproduce in angle iron. Frame Design 4 shows a similar structure.

Materials: Mild steel (ERW) tube, mild steel strip for wheel mountings - see Section 6.

Production Equipment: Cutting, drilling, welding, tube bending.

Advantages: Simplicity; low cost.

Disadvantages: Only suitable for lightweight loads; requires rigid load container.

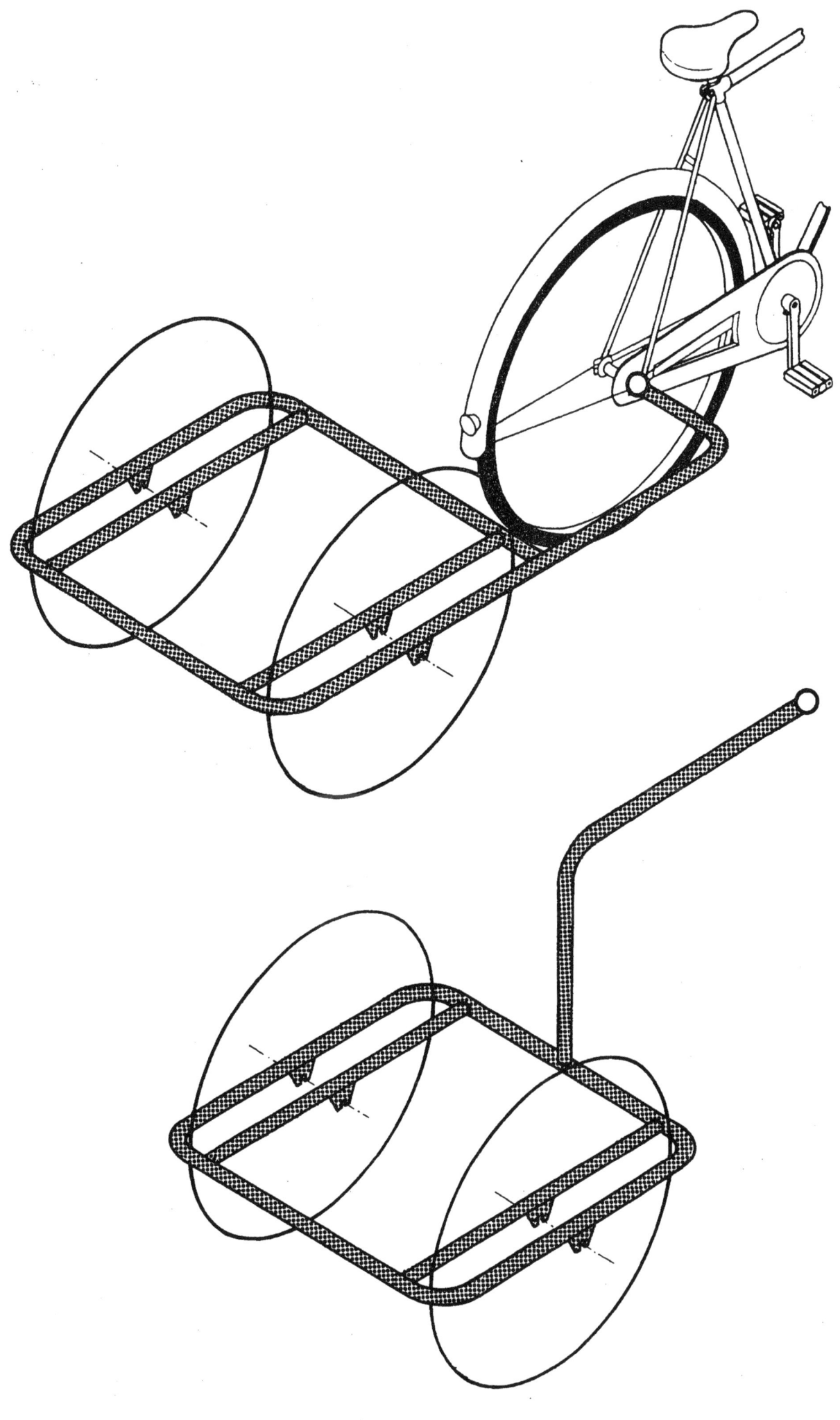

Frame Design 2 - Angled Frame

Description: This design is a common type of frame in Europe and America. Often fitted with quite small wheels (150mm - 400mm diameter), this frame is normally used for moving domestic goods. The angled configuration of the frame makes the centre of gravity of the load act just in front of the wheels. The small wheels and low ground clearance give the design a low centre of gravity and maximise stability.

To suit the requirements of developing countries, the ground clearance and size of wheels would need to be increased, and the frame construction strengthened.

Most frames of this type are produced from tubular steel, but angle iron could be substituted with minimum modification of the design.

Materials: Mild steel (ERW) tube; mild steel tube for axle (see Section 6).

Production Equipment: Cutting, welding, tube bending.

Advantages: Compact; low cost; load area not constrained by frame members.

Disadvantages: May require strong, rigid load container; design would require modification for heavy duty applications.

Commercial Examples: Cannondale; Bike Hod (see Annex 1).

Frame Design 3 - 'Loadstar' Frame

Description: This design is a heavy duty frame which was developed by I.T. Transport Ltd. as part of a programme to establish the production of cycle trailers in India.

The frame forms a rigid structure which, for some applications, can be used without a load container. The shape of the load area positions the nominal centre of gravity just in front of the wheel axle line. The frame is designed to accept standard or reinforced bicycle wheels (26" or 28"). The tow bar is a single length of tube, bent to form a 'loop' at the front of the trailer.

The outer wheel supports are reinforced by additional braces which join the base to the tow bar. This ensures that the wheels are well supported and prevents any distortion of the frame during use.

Materials: Mild steel (ERW) tube; mild steel strip for wheel mountings (see Section 6).

Production Equipment: Cutting, drilling, welding, tube bending.

Advantages: Strength of frame structure; suitability for use with simple load containers; useful as a hand cart; can be used without a load container.

Disadvantages: Reasonably complex to produce; could require a folding stand for convenient use as a hand cart.

Frame Design 4 - Angle Iron Frame

Description: This design is similar in configuration to Frame Design 3, but is constructed from angle iron. The design uses simple joints, some of which are overlapped for strength, which do not require complex angles to be cut.

As illustrated, the frame is intended for use with wheels mounted on a separate axle (see Section 6).

Materials: Mild steel angle iron; Mild steel tube for axle (see Section 6).

Production Equipment: Cutting, welding.

Advantages: Simplicity; commonly available materials; and minimum equipment requirements.

Disadvantages: Poor strength - weight ratio; unattractive appearance.

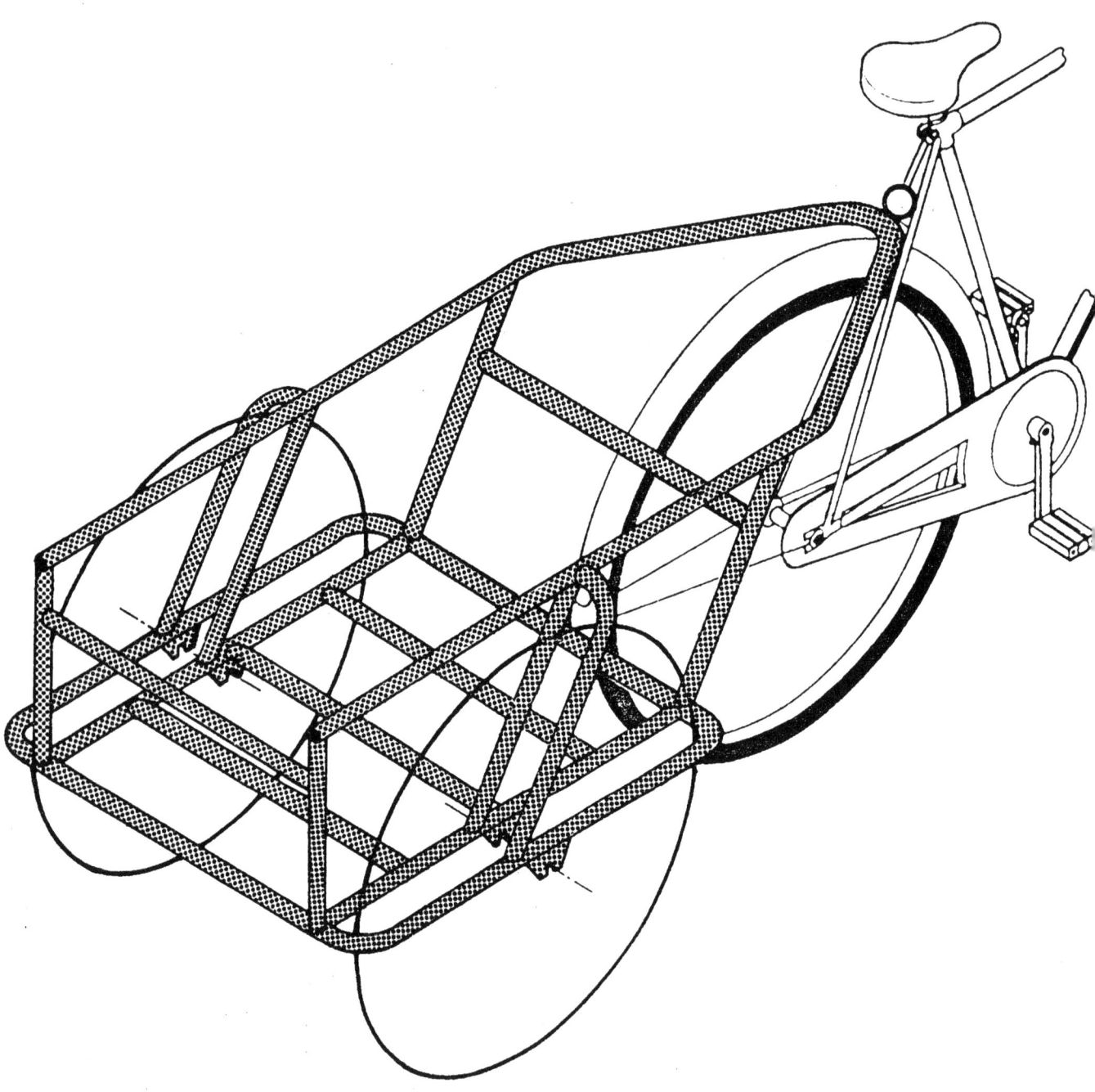

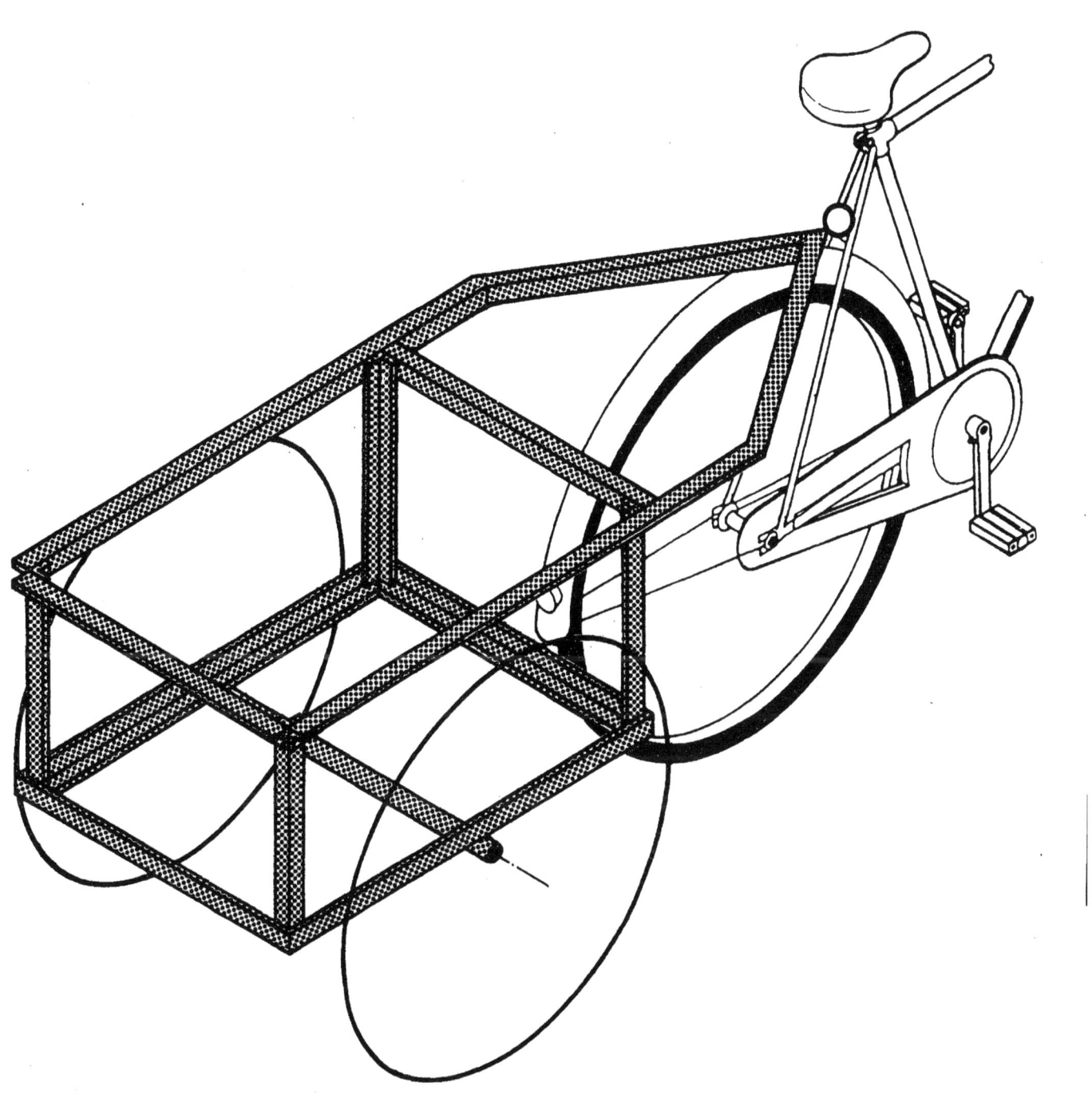

Frame Design 5 - Single Wheeled Frame

Description: This design was developed by I.T. Transport Ltd., for use with Hitch Design 8.

The frame is designed to provide a relatively small load area which does not require a container, as the capacity of the design is only 80kg. Larger loads than this are not suitable for single wheeled trailers.

The wheel is positioned at the rear of the frame to provide optimum load distribution. As illustrated, a 20" bicycle wheel is used.

The tow bar of the trailer has two frame members joined by braces. This meets the requirement for a stiff tow bar which will not flex under the high torsional loads imposed by single wheeled designs. The frame can be fitted with two handles, enabling it to be used as a hand cart. The sloping section of the tow bar allows large boxes to be carried, provided that they are tied on.

Materials: Mild steel (ERW) tube; mild steel sheet for mudguard; mild steel strip for wheel mountings (see Section 6).

Production Equipment: Cutting, welding, drilling, tube bending, sheet metal.

Advantages: Capability to operate in confined spaces or on narrow tracks and paths.

Disadvantages: Limited capacity; could be dangerous if severely over loaded.

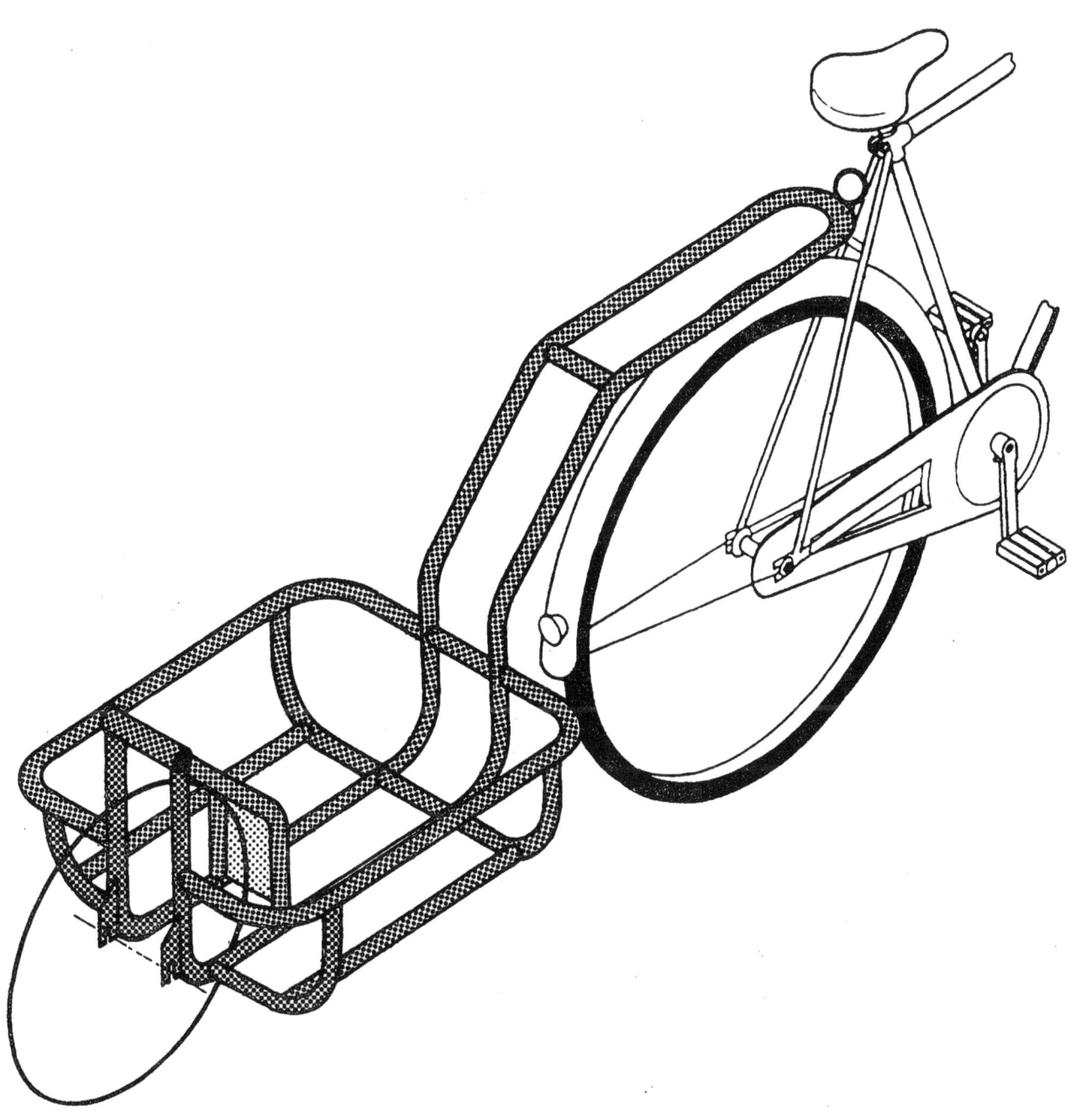

5. LOAD CONTAINERS

Introduction

The versatility of a bicycle trailer is its most important, and useful characteristic. The range of loads which can be moved with bicycle trailers is very broad, but the following suggestions may be useful:

- Farm produce.
- Liquids - water, milk, kerosene, petrol or diesel.
- Domestic goods - delivery from shop to home.
- Agricultural goods - fertiliser, etc.
- Industrial goods - components, scrap, etc.
- Street vending - drinks, etc.

Some of these applications require specialised load containers, others simply require a box. The purpose of this section is to review the options for load containers which will fit the frame designs in the previous section.

Some of the frames in the previous section offer the possibility of using interchangeable load containers. This means that one trailer can be used as a tanker - for distributing water, for example - **and** as a box trailer for collecting firewood etc. In order to realise this possibility, an integrated approach to load container design is required, which uses standard overall dimensions and matching location points.

Load Container Materials

The selection of suitable materials for a load container will depend on a number of factors including: cost; availability; strength required; and the specific application. However, there are general comments which can be made about the various options.

Matting

Locally made mats can be used for simple load containers which can fit within a frame with sides (Frame Designs 3, 4). This type of container will wear out quite quickly, but is easily and inexpensively replaced.

Wood

Wood can be used either to make a basic platform or a rigid box (see Design 2). The major disadvantage of wood is its weight. A well made, strong wooden container may be heavy, and this will increase the effort required to pull the trailer, even when it is empty.

Sheet Steel

Sheet steel is a very suitable material for load containers. It can be formed into a wide variety of shapes. Zinc coated (galvanised or GI) steel is very useful for producing drinking water tanks or containers for food, as it is resistant to rust.

However, sheet steel can be very expensive, and requires specialised equipment to form it effectively.

Glass Reinforced Plastic (GRP)

GRP, commonly referred to as 'Fibreglass', is a very useful material for load containers, but it is not widely available in most developing countries, and is often expensive. However, it is very useful for producing insulated containers or tanks for carrying drinkable liquids (milk, water) or unpackaged food. The production processes used to make GRP containers naturally provide smooth surfaces and well-rounded corners, making them easy to clean.

Load Container Designs

The following designs are examples of load containers which have been developed for locally produced trailers in various developing countries.

The information in this section is presented in the following way:

- A detailed drawing of each container.

- A description of each load container.

- A list of materials and components required.

- A brief analysis of each design which notes advantages and disadvantages.

The information in this section should be combined with data in Sections 2, 3, 4 and 6 to select or develop a suitable trailer design.

Load Container Design 1 - Sheet Steel Box

Description:
This design was developed by I.T. Transport Ltd. as part of a programme to establish the production of cycle trailers in India. As illustrated, it is designed to fit Frame Design 3. However, the concept of a sheet metal box container is very simple, and the shape illustrated can be easily modified.

Sheet metal containers of this type are only suited to frames which have considerable side support, as the container itself is not rigid. The container illustrated was made from 0.7mm (22 gauge SWG) steel sheet. In tests, this has proved suitable, provided that the container is well supported by the frame. The joints on the container can be welded or rivetted. This type of container can be welded to the frame if a permanent mounting is required. However, if inter-changeable containers are to be used, or repairs required, it may be better to use self tapping screws, which will allow for quick removal.

Materials/Components
Mild steel sheet 0.7mm (22 SWG); rivets for joints (if required); self tapping screws for attaching container to frame.

Production Equipment:
Shearing, folding, spot welding, (use of this equipment will enable a high quality container to be made. Simple containers can be made using hand folding techniques and rivets).

Advantages: Light; strong; durable; easily removed from frame.

Disadvantages: Needs support from frame; can be expensive.

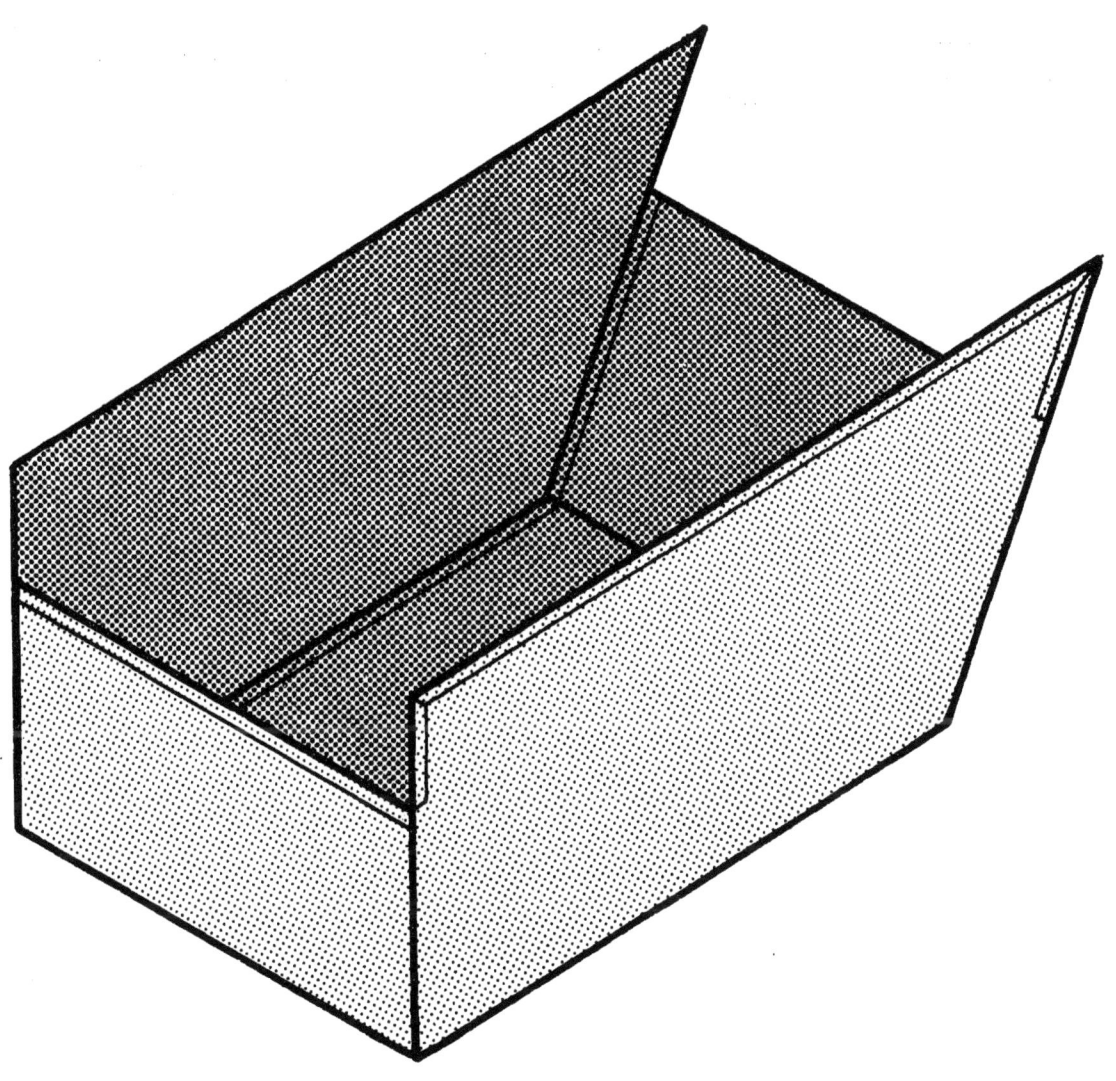

Load Container Design 2 - Wooden Box

Description: The concept of this design is significantly different from the previous example in that it does not require side support. The box can be attached to the base of the trailer frame using nuts and bolts. It can be easily removed if inter-changeable containers are required. In order to provide sufficient strength, the box needs to be constructed from wood - either sheets of plywood, etc. or planks - at least 15mm thick. It also requires strong corner braces. These braces should be screwed and glued to the sides.

This type of container can be provided with a folding tail gate to facilitate loading and unloading, but this will reduce the overall rigidity of the structure unless the catches which hold the tailgate in the closed position are well designed and securely located. Box containers can also be fitted with lids to increase the security of the cargo.

Materials/
Components   Wood for sides and base (plywood or local timber), at least 15mm thick; braces, approximately 50mm square section; screws; glue; nuts, bolts and washers for attaching container to the trailer frame.

Production
Equipment: Handtools - saw, drill, screwdriver.

Advantages: Low cost (if locally produced wood is used); simplicity; easy removal from frame.

Disadvantages: Weight; poor durability if not properly constructed.

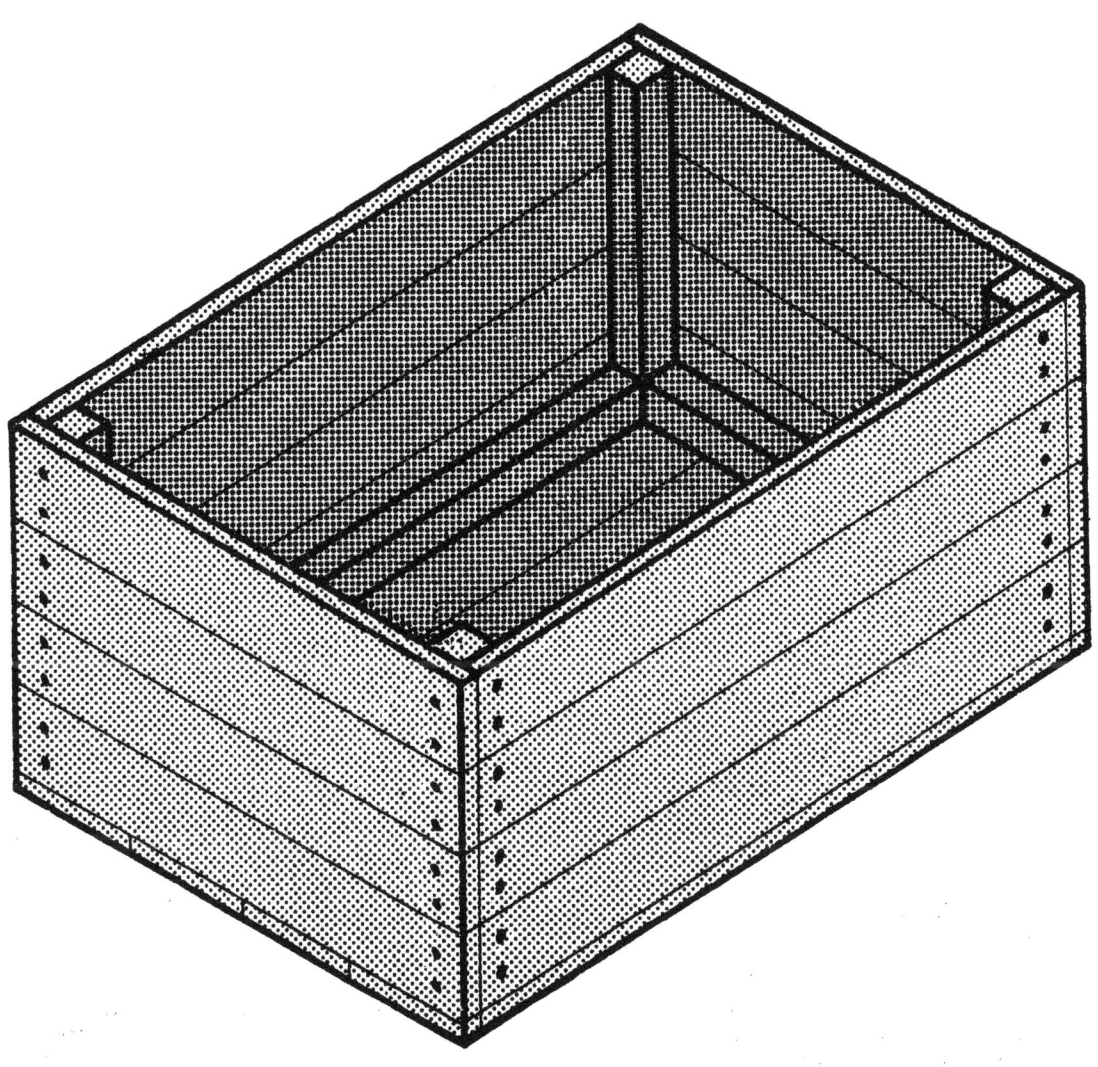

Load Container Design 3 - Tank

Description: Tanks can be used to transport a range of liquids - kerosene, oil, petrol, agricultural chemicals and water. The design shown can be made from galvanised steel sheet if a clean container for drinking water is required. If the trailer frame is a suitable size, the tank can be produced by modifying a standard 200 litre oil drum. This modification requires a cap to be added to the top of the tank, in order to facilitate the filling of the container. A further modification, which is worth including in any fabricated container, is to include a 'baffle'. A baffle is a plate, built into the tank. It prevents rapid movement of the liquid from one end of the container to the other, which can affect the handling and balance of the bicycle. A gap must be left at the bottom of the baffle to allow the tank to be emptied. A standard tap fitting, attached to the rear of the tank, allows liquids to be emptied easily.

A cradle fitted to the tank will allow it to be easily attached to or detached from the trailer frame and ensure that it is held in the correct position. Alternatively, it can be retained by the frame, as in Frame Design 3.

Materials/
Components   Mild steel or galvanised (GI) sheet - 0.5mm or 0.7mm thick (24 or 22 SWG); tap fitting; mild steel strip for cradle; nuts, bolts and washers.

Production
Equipment: Sheet metal rolling and shearing equipment; welding; drilling; cutting.

Advantages: Versatile container that can carry a range of liquids; easily removed.

Disadvantages: Reasonably complex to fabricate.

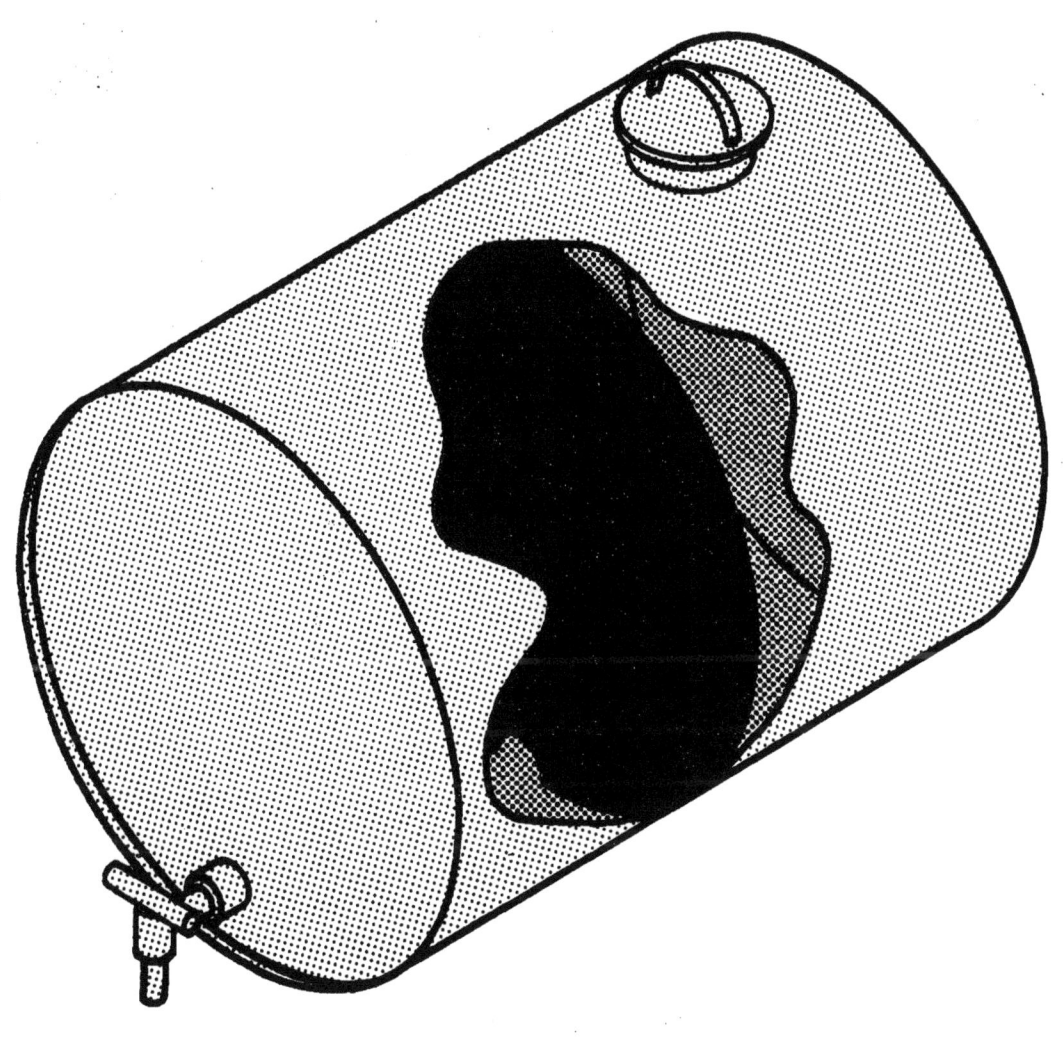

Load Container Design 4 - Insulated Box

Description: Insulated boxes fitted with lids can be used for distributing and selling a range of perishable goods, including milk, ice cream, cold drinks, etc. The design illustrated is made of Glass Reinforced Plastic (GRP). The material is well suited to this application, as the internal surfaces can be easily cleaned; wood or steel can also be used. The important feature of insulated boxes is the space between the inner and outer containers which is filled with material which slows down the change of temperature of the load. Polystyrene foam (used for packing fragile products) is a good material, but may be difficult to obtain. Sacking, scraps of cloth or wood shavings, etc. are possible substitutes. This type of container should be constructed so that it can be easily removed from the trailer. This will enable other loads to be moved if the transport of perishable loads is a seasonal requirement.

Materials/
Components: GRP (matting, resin, material for moulds); or wood/steel sheet; insulating material; fittings for lid; nuts, bolts and washers for attaching container to frame.

Production
Equipment: GRP moulding facilities and steel/woodworking equipment - cutting, welding; drilling.

Advantages: Effective transport/distribution of perishable goods; easily removed from frame.

Disadvantages: Can be complex to construct; reasonably heavy.

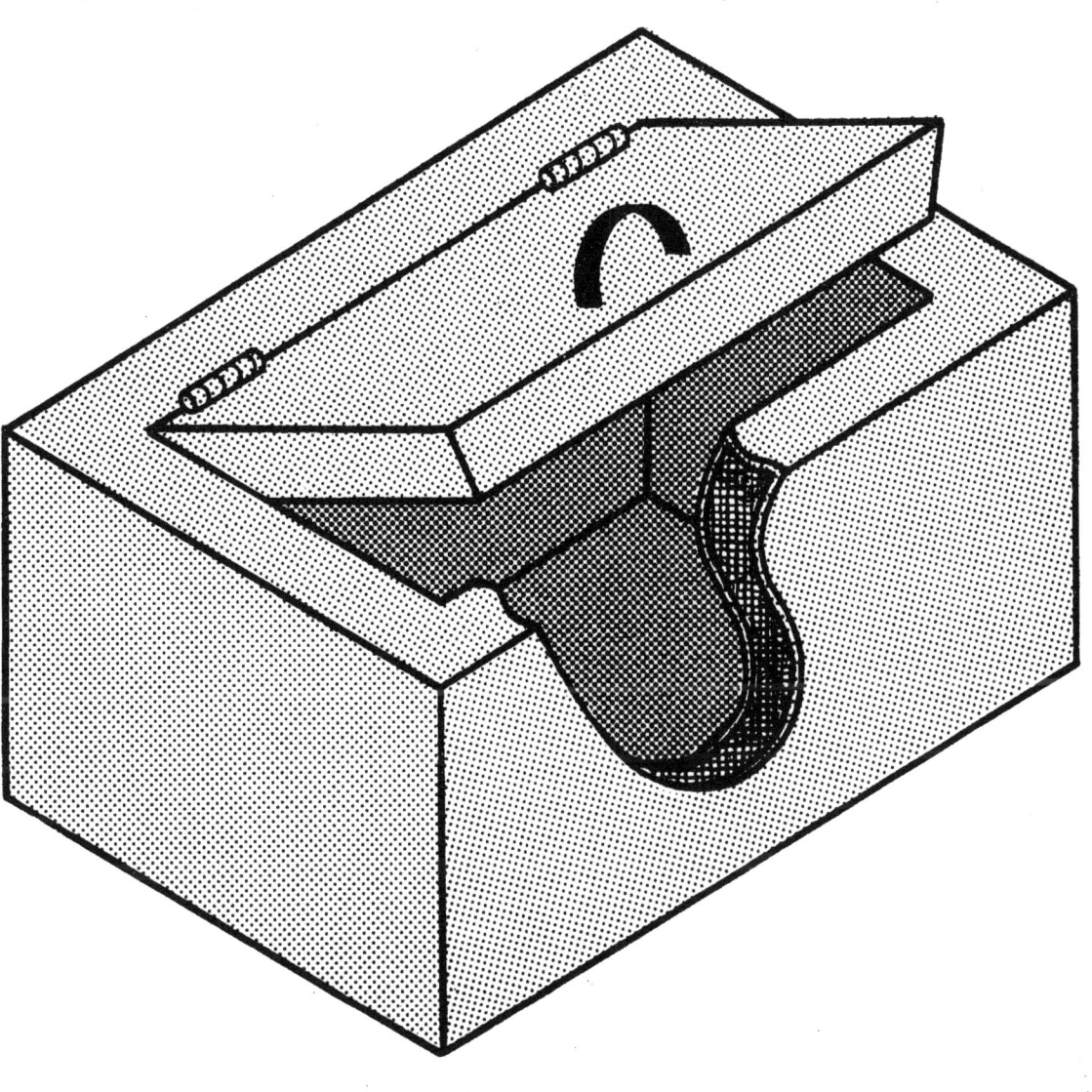

6. WHEELS

Introduction

The wheels are likely to be the most expensive part of any bicycle trailer, and they are certainly the most easily damaged. The purpose of this section is to look at some of the factors which affect the specification of bicycle trailer wheels, review alternative methods of attaching the wheels to the frame, and examine wheel designs which are commercially available or suitable for local manufacture.

Requirements - Bicycle Trailer Wheels

The technical requirements of wheels for a bicycle trailer will depend on the weight to be carried, the condition of the road or track which will be used, and on the care that is exercised by the user. For a two wheeled trailer which is likely to be heavily and consistently over-loaded, each wheel should be able to support 180kg (see Section 1). This type of use suggests a lack of care by the user, and a further allowance should be made for careless riding on rough roads. This is, however, an extreme example, and the majority of trailers will carry considerably smaller loads (150 - 200kg maximum). The technical requirements for each wheel on a two wheeled trailer can, therefore, be estimated as follows:

- Capable of supporting a load of 75 - 100kg.
- Capable of withstanding shock and axial loads imposed by rough ground and pot holes.
- Made from locally available components.
- Capable of repair using locally available facilities.
- Low friction bearings in the hubs.

The cost of the wheels used on the trailer will have a significant influence on the overall price of the product. For example, motor cycle wheels are durable and capable of supporting considerable loads, but prohibitively expensive for a bicycle trailer, unless scrap wheels can be obtained and re-built cheaply. In practice a compromise between the cost and technical suitability of wheels has to be reached, depending on the importance attached to each requirement.

Attachment of Wheels to the Frame

On a two wheeled bicycle trailer, the wheels must rotate independantly of each other. There are two basic methods of achieving this.

The first method is to attach each wheel independently, using slotted plates similar to those used on bicycle forks (Figure 6.1). This method is used on some of the trailer frames shown in Section 4. Using slotted plates allows each wheel to be removed independently for repair or maintenance. Another advantage of this method is that the frame member which supports the outside of the wheel also acts as a protective guard. This can be very useful in congested areas, where there is a possibility of the trailer wheel catching on people or other vehicles.

The second method is to attach the wheels to a fixed axle. If this method is used, the axle forms part of the trailer frame (see Frame Design 4). The wheels rotate on the ends of the axle, which has to be turned on a lathe to accept bearings or plain bushes (Figure 6.2).

This type of axle has an overhanging or cantilevered section which supports the wheel. The loads which will be imposed on the wheel must be carefully estimated in order to specify the correct diameter and material for the axle. Failure to do this may result in the axle bending or shearing off.

A method of retaining the wheel on the axle also needs to be provided. This is usually achieved by a nut and a split pin which slots through a location hole drilled through the axle.

Another version of this method, which uses less material but requires very high standards of specification, accuracy, and welding is to attach stub axles to the trailer frame. These are short axles which are welded to each side of the frame. They have the advantage that they can be positioned virtually anywhere on the side of the frame, but need to be located securely and very accurately to ensure efficient and safe operation of the trailer.

Commercially Available Wheels

In specifying wheels for trailers the obvious starting point is to use standard bicycle wheels. However, bicycle wheels have a number of drawbacks when used on trailers:

- They can be relatively expensive, often constituting 50% or more of the total cost of the trailer.

- Their strength is marginal for use on a heavily loaded trailer. This is partly due to the considerable loads which can be carried, but also to the basic layout of a two wheeled trailer, which imposes considerably greater side loads on the wheels than they have to withstand when used on a bicycle.

Set against their deficiencies, however, are considerable benefits. Bicycle wheels are locally available and easily repaired in most developing countries. They are lightweight and, because they have a large diameter and are fitted with pneumatic tyres, are very efficient.

The standard developing country bicycle wheel has a diameter of 26" or 28" (660 or 710mm) and a rim width of 1.5" (37.5mm). In addition 20" (550mm) diameter by 1.75" or 2" (45 or 50mm) bicycle wheels are available in several developing countries. 20" wheels are very suitable for use on bicycle trailers, as the relatively small diameter makes them resistant to the side loads which are generated by normal use on rough roads. It is recommended that wheels less than 20" (500mm) in diameter should not be used on bicycle trailers in developing countries, as the rolling resistance would be too great and the capability to roll over obstructions too small. However, the majority

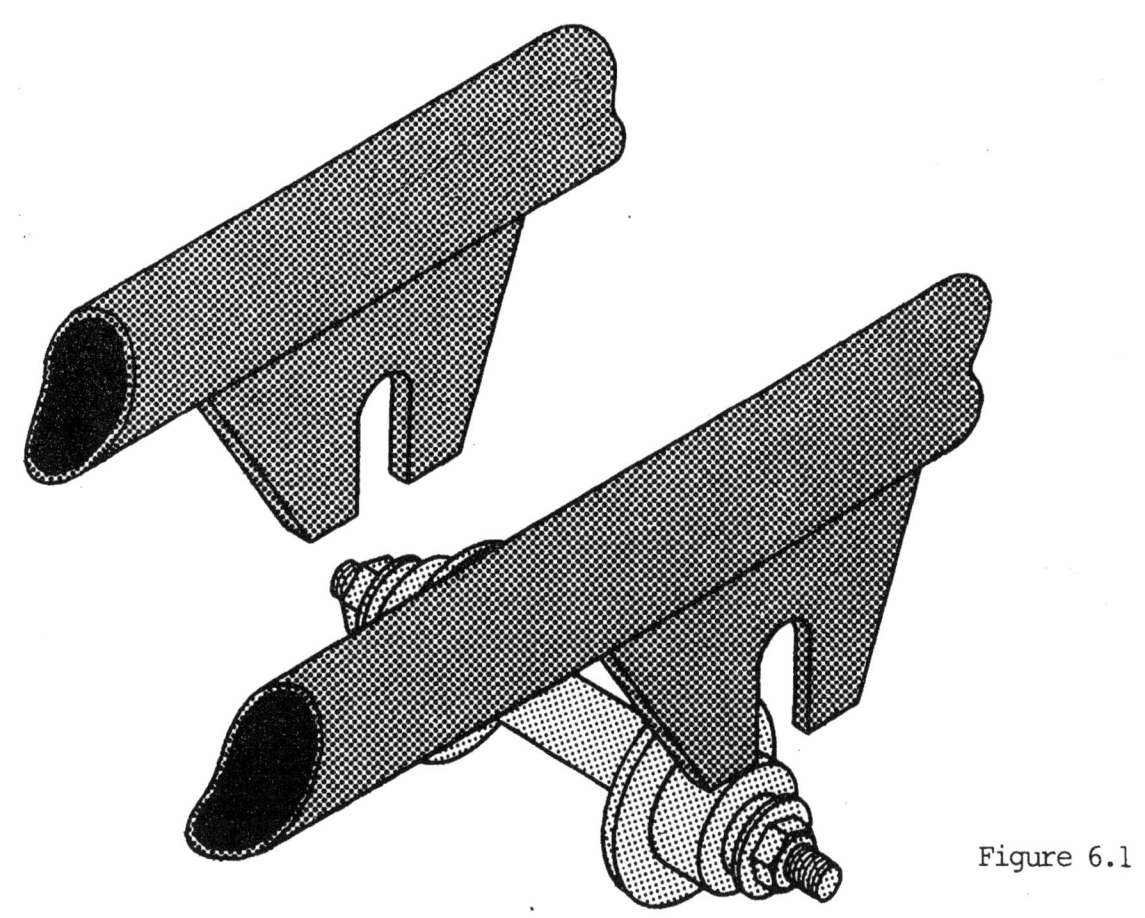

Figure 6.1

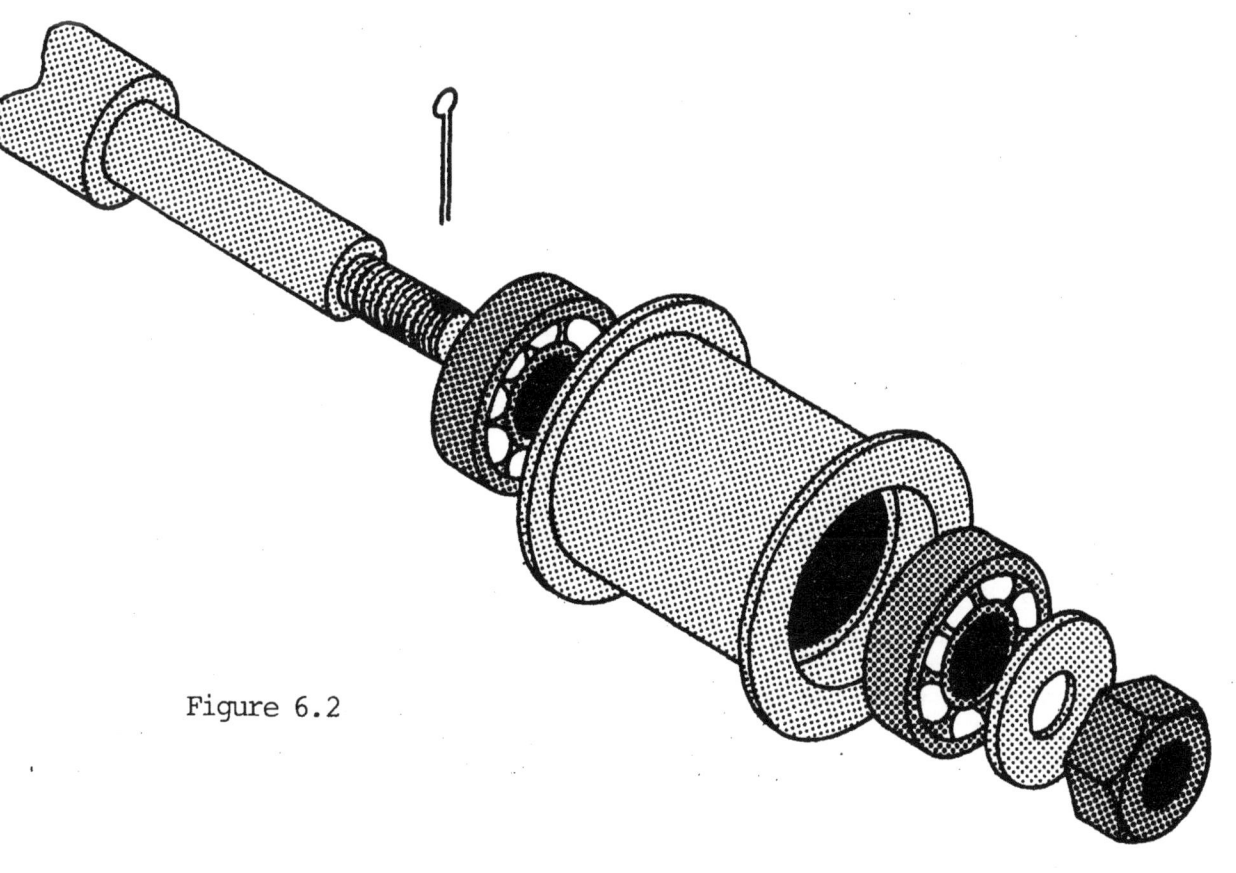

Figure 6.2

of trailers will need to be fitted with the larger (26" or 28") diameter bicycle wheels, as these are by far the most commonly available sizes throughout the world.

In some countries the strength of bicycle wheels can be significantly increased using locally available components. This is particularly true in the Indian sub continent, where several methods for strengthening bicycle wheels are commercially available. These can be summarised as follows:

- Reinforced rims are available which improve the rigidity and strength of the wheel.

- 64 spoke hubs and rims are produced in addition to the standard 32 spoke (front wheel) and 40 spoke (rear wheel) components.

- 12 or 10 gauge (2.6mm or 3.2mm) spokes are produced in addition to standard 14 gauge (2.0mm) spokes.

- Machined hubs are available which will accept ball bearings and can be used with standard spokes and rims. This type of hub is suitable for mounting on a fixed axle.

Annex 1 gives lists of suppliers of bicycle components. It is likely that some or all of these heavy duty components can be obtained from the suppliers listed in India.

Assuming it is not possible to obtain or produce heavy duty components, the most suitable wheel that can be made using standard parts will have the following specification:

- 26" or 28" rim, tyre and tube.

- 40, 14 gauge (2.0mm) spokes.

- 40 spoke hub (rear wheel).

- 3/8" (9.5mm) axle.

The most important factor which affects the ability of a normal spoked wheel to resist damage is correct construction and maintenance. If spokes are loose or improperly tensioned, the overall structure of the wheel will be weakened. Similarly, if a broken or loose spoke is not repaired, the wheel will rapidly deteriorate, and may suddenly collapse.

Pneumatic tyres are very efficient, but prone to punctures. There are a number of techniques and products which can make conventional tyres puncture resistant or replace the tyre with a puncture proof substitute. Annex 1 gives data on two commercially available products which reduce the incidence of punctures - one by providing a protective band between the tyre and the tube, the other by use of a viscous fluid that seals the tyre from the inside when small objects penetrate the inner tube. A study of these products, and other techniques suitable for local production is referred to in Annex 2.

Wheel Designs

The alternative to using commercially available wheels is to produce a design locally. Wheels are, however, complex devices - particularly if light weight is to be combined with strength and durability. Both these requirements are essential for an efficient bicycle trailer, and the range of designs for local manufacture is, therefore, limited. The following designs are proven technologies which use different types of tyre and require different levels of technical capability. The information is presented in the following way:

- Diagrams showing the construction of each wheel.

- A description of the production technology of each wheel.

- A list of materials and components required.

- A list of production equipment needed.

- A brief analysis of each design which notes advantages and disadvantages.

Wheel Design 1 - Split Rim Wheel

Description: The split rim wheel was developed by I.T. Transport Ltd. from a concept originally used on motor scooters and animal carts. The wheel is suitable for use with either 20" bicycle tyres or moped tyres. The split rim allows the wheel to be assembled around the tyre and tube. It can therefore be maintained and repaired without specialised pneumatic tyre equipment.

The rim is made of two lengths of mild steel strip with tube or rod welded around the circumference to retain the tyre. Spokes are welded to one half of the rim, and tabs to the other. Bolts are used to join the two halves. Semi circular cuts in each half of the rim locate the inner tube valve.

The hub can be machined to provide locations for ball bearings or fitted with a plain bush made of cast iron, nylon, etc.

Materials/
Components: Mild steel strip (approximately 25 mm wide for moped tyres and 18mm wide for 20" x 2" bicycle tyres); mild steel round bar or tube (approximately 8mm diameter) to retain tyre; mild steel tube (18mm x 2.5 - 4mm) for spokes; mild steel tube for hub; bearings or plain bushes.

Equipment: Cutting, welding, drilling.

Advantages: Reasonably simple to construct; uses a pneumatic tyre; reasonably light in weight.

Disadvantages: Requires access to tyre supplies, needs to be accurately constructed.

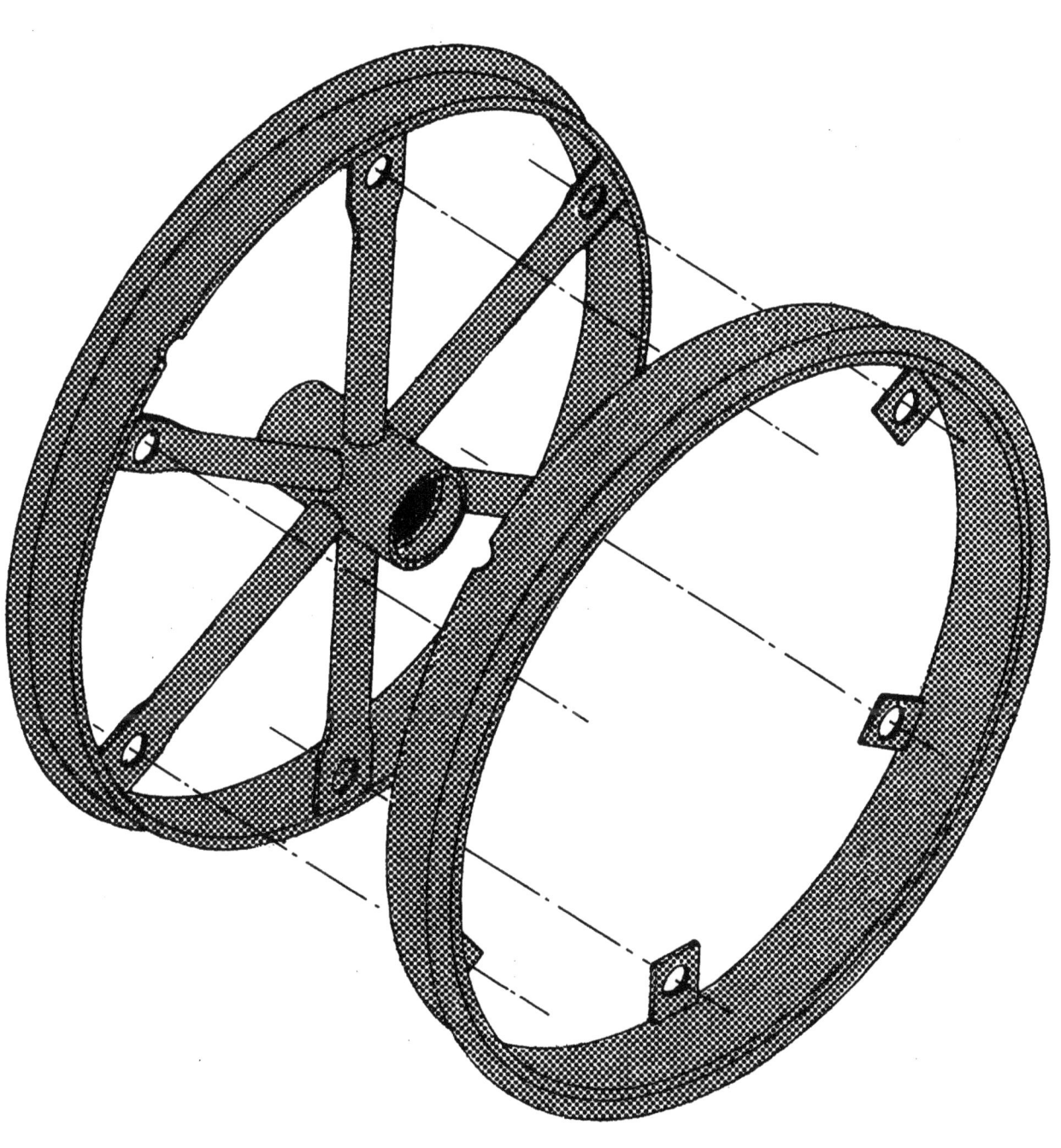

Wheel Design 2 - Solid Rubber Tyred Wheel

Description: This design is a low cost wheel which is available in some parts of India. These wheels are usually fitted to small handcarts, and are best suited to low speed use on trailers, as the solid rubber tyre has poorer performance characteristics than a pneumatic tyre. The wheels are made by small workshops, and require considerable skill unless production tooling is developed to locate the parts prior to welding. The tyre is cut from scrap motor vehicle - usually truck - tyres. The rim is hand formed from sheet steel into a section which, once hammered around the tyre, holds it securely in place. This is the most difficult part of the construction, and requires good blacksmithing skills.

The spokes are formed as 'U' shaped rods, which loop through the hub. The spokes are located in holes in the rim and welded on both sides. At the hub, the 'double spokes' loop through and are welded to, the flanges, creating a strong and very durable joint. Hubs can be made from steel tube to accept plain, ball or roller bearings.

Materials/
Components: Mild steel sheet - approximately 2.0mm - 2.6mm thick (14 - 12 gauge); mild steel round bar (approximately 8mm diameter); scrap car or truck tyre; mild steel tube; mild steel strip.

Equipment: Cutting, welding, drilling, metal bending.

Advantages: Can be made in a wide range of sizes; does not require a pneumatic tyre; uses locally available parts.

Disadvantages: Rim fabrication requires considerable skill; reasonably heavy; solid rubber tyre creates greater rolling resistance than a pneumatic tyre.

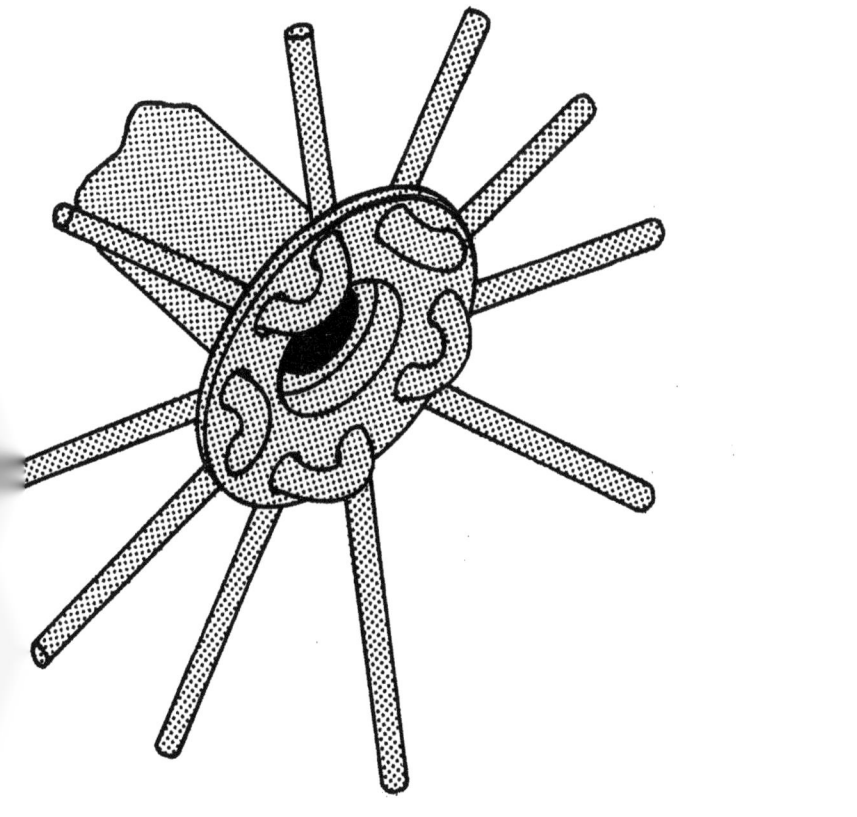

7. USE OF BICYCLE TRAILERS

Introduction

Some of the factors affecting the use of bicycle trailers are discussed in the introductory sections. However, most of these are worthy of further emphasis, and other issues have not been discussed. The purpose of this section, therefore, is to review some simple techniques and precautions which will help to ensure that bicycle trailers perform safely and effectively.

Loading and Unloading

The suggested maximum loads for bicycle trailers are:

    150kg - Two wheeled trailer
    80kg - Single wheeled trailer

It is recognised that in practice, these theoretical maximums will be exceeded. This should be considered during the design process, by including suitable safety factors for critical components, but should not result in an excessively heavy design.

Safe loading involves placing the load as near as possible to the axle line of the trailer. If this is not possible, the load should be biased in front of the axle line. Loads which may move during transit should be tied on - particularly if they are heavy - as sudden movement in the trailer could throw the rider off the bicycle. Very high loads should be avoided, as these will make the trailer unstable.

Stability

The stability of a bicycle trailer is adversely affected by:

- Cornering too quickly.
- Travelling too fast over very rough ground.
- Turning very sharp corners.

The extent to which these will affect the stability of a trailer will be conditioned by the amount of load being carried. If the trailer is empty, some care will be required when using it, at least until experience is developed.

Maintenance

The part of the trailer which requires the most frequent maintenance is the hitch mechanism. The most important checks are:

- Grease on all the moving parts of the mechanical designs.
- Tightness and alignment of the connection between the cycle and the hitch.

- Degree of 'snatch' in the hitch - this should be kept to a minimum.

- Condition of the pin, if any, which secures the trailer to the hitch.

Wheels also require regular checks on the bearings, spokes, tyres and rims. Failure to do this may result in sudden - and dangerous - wheel failure.

Annex 1: Commercial Suppliers of Bicycle Trailers and Components

Bicycle Trailer Manufacturers

The following list is not exhaustive, but provides basic contact data on bicycle trailer manufacturers in different parts of the world.

Manufacturer	Product Comment
Bike Hod Ltd., 29 Leslie Park Road, Croydon, Surrey, CRO 6TN, UK.	Developed Hitch Design 1. Market a trailer similar to Frame Design 2 but the standard wheels are probably too small (300mm diameter) for use in developing countries.
Woodland World Limited. Shirehill Works, Saffron Walden, Essex, UK.	Developed Hitch Design 7. Market the 'Shuttle' Trailer in the UK. Uses a GRP load container.
Pearsons, Sutton, Surrey, UK.	Two designs similar to Frame Design 2. Light-weight Camping/Shopping trailers.
Cleminsons Agencies Ltd., St. Johns Street, Huntingdon, Cambridgeshire, UK.	Croysdale Trailer. Platform frame, similar to Frame Design 1, which can be fitted with different load containers. Simple ball and socket hitch Light-weight construction.
Cannondale Corporation, 35 Pulaski Street, Stamford, Connecticut, USA.	Similar to Frame Design 2. Has larger wheels than the Bike Hod. Mainly intended for camping - light weight frame.
Blue Sky Cycle Carts, 29976 Enid Road East, Eugene, Oregon 97402, USA.	Designers of Hitch Design 4. Market a platform frame design which can be fitted with various load containers. Trailer is fitted with large wheels.
Batavus Cycles, Netherlands.	Innovative, collapsible frame. Useful for storage in restricted areas. 20" wheels, light-weight construction.
Malindi Rural Centre, Malawi.	Steel framed trailer (similar to Frame Designs 3 and 4). Uses 20" diameter wheels.

Bicycle Trailer Components

The following list provides some basic contact data on manufacturers of bicycle components required for trailers. The data is divided into two sections:

- A list of companies and the components produced.
- Contact details for the companies.

Manufacturer / Component	Wheel Rims	Spokes/ Nipples	Tyres/ Tubes	Wheel Hubs	Protective Tyre Inserts	Puncture Sealants
USA						
Hi-E Engineering	X			X		
Schwinn	X		X			
Torrington		X				
Windsor	X		X			
Mr. Tuffy					X	
FRANCE						
Hutchinson			X			
Maillard				X		
Perrin				X		
Rousson				X		
Dunlop			X			
Wolber			X			
Velox			X			
Chimiplast			X			
LFT	X					
ITALY						
Ofmega				X		
Artar				X		
Campagnolo				X		
Gipiemme				X		
Faini		X				
Rizzato	X					
SPAIN						
Artexim	X	X				
Beistegui	X					
Camaneiro	X					
Akrent	X					
Zeus	X					
Pirelli			X			

Manufacturer \ Component	Wheel Rims	Spokes/ Nipples	Tyres/ Tubes	Wheel Hubs	Protective Tyre Inserts	Puncture Sealants
UK						
T.I. Raleigh		X		X		
Lemet Metal Works		X				
Hipkiss Wire Products		X				
Michelin			X			
H+M						X
OKO						X
WEST GERMANY						
Weco				X		
Schurmann	X					
Union		X		X		
Fichtel + Sacks				X		
INDIA						
Federal Sports		X				
Hero Cycles	X			X		
T.I. Cycles	X			X		

Manufacturers' Addresses

USA

Blue Sky Cycle Carts,
29976 Enid Road East,
Eugene,
Oregon 97402.

HI-E Engineering Inc.,
1247 School Lane,
Nashville,
Tennessee 37217.

Mr. Tuffy Co.,
20 Old Squan Plaza,
Manasquan,
NJ 08736.

Schwinn Bicycle Co.,
1856 N. Kostner Ave.,
Chicago,
Illinoi 60616.

The Torrington Company,
Cycle Parts Div.,
Torrington,
Conn. 06790.

Windsor Enterprises Inc.,
2702 S. Port Way,
Unit A & B,
Corner of 28 West St.,
National City,
California 92050.

FRANCE

Chimiplast,
60 rue Saint-Denis,
93300 Neuilly-Sur-Seine.

Dunlop,
Tour Atlantique,
92800 Puteaux.

Hutchinson - MAPA Cycles,
124 av. des Champs-Elysees,
2 rue Balzac,
75008 Paris,
BP 762.08-75360.

Laminiors A Froid De Thionville
   (LFT),
Route de Manom,
BP 50, 57101 Thionville.

Maillard,
76117 Incheville,
BP 1-75117 Incheville.

Perrin - Usine de Lardy,
BP 29,
42130 Leigneux par Boen-Sur-Lignon.

Rousson & Charmoux,
rue Parmentier,
BP 4-42110 FEURS.

Velox,
29 bis,
rue Jean-Moulin,
95100 Argenteuil.

Wolber,
17 rue de Villeneuve,
BP 6-0221 Soissons.

ITALY

Artar Spa,
Via Marzalesco,
Cureggio.

Campagnolo Brevetti Internaz Spa,
C.so Padova 168,
Vicenza.

Faini Federico Srl,
Maggianico Sco E. Filiberto 74,
Lecco.

Gipiemme Srl,
Via Vicenza,
Camisano Vicentino.

OF.ME.GA Component Speciali,
Via G. Gozzano,
Sarezzo.

Rizzato Cesare E.C. Spa,
Via Venezia, 29,
Padova.

SPAIN

Artexim S.A.,
Rambia Cataluna,
115 bis,
11.A Edificio Catalonia,
Barcelona-8.

Beistegui Hermanos, SA,
Arcacha, s/n,
Victoria.

Camaneiro S.A.,
Francisco Marti Mora, 1,
Edificio (Bldg.),
Torre, Palma De Mallorca.

Manufacturas Akrent, S.A.,
Riera dels Frares,
3-5-7 Hospitalet de Llobregat,
Barcelona.

Pirelli Productos, S.A.,
Avda. Jose Antonio, 612,
Barcelona-7.

Zeus Industrial S.A.,
Barrio Matiena, s/n,
Abadiano (Vizcaya)

UNITED KINGDOM

H+M Products Ltd.,
PO Box 101,
London,
SE9 6TQ.

Hipkiss Wire Products,
Goodman Street Works,
Birmingham,
B1 2SU.

Lemet Metal Works,
Delta Way,
Watling Street,
Bridgtown,
Cannock,
SW11 3BE.

Michelin Tyre Co. Ltd.,
81 Fulham Road,
London,
SW3 6RD.

OKO International,
Tongstyle Ltd.,
Brookside,
Sandalheath Ind. Estate,
Fordingbridge,
Hants.

T.I. Raleigh Ltd.,
177 Lenton Boulevard,
Nottingham.
NG7 2DD.

WEST GERMANY

Fichtel + Sachs,
AF, Ernst-Sachs-Strasse 62,
D-8720 Schweinfurt.

Schurmann-Werk,
Fritz Schurmann GmbH & Co. KG,
Postfach 1209,
D-4811 Leopoldshone 1.

Union Sils,
Van de Loo & Co.,
Wilhelm-Feuerhake-Str. 7,
D-5758 Frondenberg/Ruhr.

Weco-Werke,
Postfach 1170,
4806 Werther b. Bielefeld.

INDIA

Federal Sports,
20/1 Asaf Ali Road,
New Delhi.

Hero Cycles Pvt. Ltd.,
GT Road,
Ludhiana.

T.I. Cycles of India Ltd.,
11-12 North Beach Road,
Madras-1.

Annex 2: Further Reading

The following publications will provide useful data on a range of issues related to bicycle trailers - specific trailer designs; bicycle design; wheel construction; puncture prevention; etc.

1. AYRE, M and HATHWAY, G.K. How to Make a Bicycle Ambulance. 1984 (Intermediate Technology Development Group Ltd.).

2. AYRE, M and BARWELL, I.J. Puncture Prevention Techniques for Pneumatic Tyres. (Forthcoming publication from the Intermediate Technology Development Group Ltd.).

3. WHITT, F.R. and WILSON, D.G. Bicycling Science - Ergonomics and Mechanics. 1974. (MIT Press).

4. BRANDT, J. The Bicycle Wheel. 1981. (Avocet, Inc. California, USA).

5. HATHWAY, G.K. Low-Cost Vehicles: Options for Moving People and Goods. 1984. (Intermediate Technology Publications Ltd.).

www.ingramcontent.com/pod-product-compliance
Ingram Content Group UK Ltd.
Pitfield, Milton Keynes, MK11 3LW, UK
UKHW050227150426
5217IPUK00024B/1679